Choosing the Green?

Second Generation Irish and the Cause of Ireland

Brian Dooley

For Esther Dooley,
born in Dublin on Thursday, September 13, 2001

First published 2004
by
Beyond the Pale
BTP Publications Ltd
Unit 2.1.2 Conway Mill
5-7 Conway Street
Belfast BT13 2DE

Tel: +44 (0)28 90 438630
Fax: +44 (0)28 90 439707
E-mail: office@btpale.com
Website: http://www.btpale.com

British Library Cataloguing-in-Publication Data.
A catalogue record for this book is available from the British Library.

ISBN 1-900960-26-5

Printed in Dublin by Colour Books Ltd.

Contents

Acknowledgements

It's fairly usual for authors to open their acknowledgements with a heartfelt thanks to the such-and-such trust or the so-and-so foundation that funded their research, or at least the academic institution that provided the time and space, and sometimes a fellowship, to complete their project. This book was written without the benefits of such resources – none were offered, and none sought.

It took several years of whatever 'spare' time I could find between doing a full-time job and bringing up a baby, and I paid for all travel, phone and other expenses myself. I include this information not in any bid for canonisation, but to encourage others daunted by the prospect of embarking on a book project without the advantages of a full-time academic career. It is possible if you are prepared to take your time, can find an understanding publisher, and have the support of a great family.

That said, this book depended on many people who helped me find contacts. These include Joe Bradley, Kieran Clifford, Alastair Logan, Martín MacOiste, Padraig Ó Cuanacháin and Maurice Quinlivan.

Others who helped include Shane O'Neill at the Irish Post, who sent me important archive material. Michael Crowley read parts of the manuscript and offered incisive advice, while Jim Doherty scoured his brain for details of his glamorous showband career in 1980s Kilburn. Conor Foley shared his experiences under the Prevention of Terrorism Act (PTA) with me, and Paddy Hillyard was also enormously helpful in his analysis of how many second generation Irish people were included in his landmark study of the PTA. Ursula Fraser explained the intricacies of nationality under Irish constitutional law, and Brian Ruane offered an objective and valuable analysis of Seán MacStiofáin's Irish language accent.

I'd also like to thank those people who agreed to be interviewed. Without them it would have been impossible to write this book. They include Margaret Brady, Kieran Clifford, Kevin Day, Pat Doherty MP, Ellen Duncan, Dr Garret Fitzgerald, Michael Gallagher, Paddy Kelly, Martin McNamara, Vince, John and Pat Maguire, Jimmy Murphy, Theresa Moriarty, Sean Ó Ceallacháin and the late Seán MacStiofáin, whom I spent many hours interviewing not long before his death.

A very special thanks to Alison, for putting up with it all again. It's time she wrote a book about living with someone who's writing a book.

Introduction

I had to spend the afternoon of Saturday October 7, 2000 at a meeting in my office in Dublin while Kerry were playing Galway in the All-Ireland Football Championship final replay. I desperately wanted to see the end of the match, and rushed into the nearest bar just as a crowd pushed its way out the door, the game obviously having just finished. 'What was the score?' I asked the nearest person. 'Hahaha,' he shouted at me in a Dublin accent. 'You lost, you lost' and pointed up at the giant screen, which said ENGLAND 0, GERMANY 1 in a world cup qualifier.

He had wrongly assumed all sorts of things from my London accent – that I didn't follow GAA, that I wasn't Irish, that I supported the England football team. 'Wait,' I wanted to shout back, 'my cousin Paddy Bawn Brosnan was a famous player in the great Kerry teams of the 1940s. I played Gaelic football for London. I live here. I've got an Irish passport…' But he was gone, and I wouldn't have said any of that anyway. As second generation Irish people know, those conversations are humiliating and risky.

These struggles with Irishness go back to my school days in the 1970s. Most of my south London school-mates had Irish parents who had settled in England in the 1940s and 1950s, but we had been born and raised in London. Did that make us English or Irish? Most of us made regular summer trips to Ireland, looked Irish, even knew a few Irish words. Some of us just felt Irish - all our relations were Irish, as were most of our parents' friends, our priests and our teachers.

But identifying yourself as Irish was problematic. The IRA was attacking London and the explosions forced us to choose whose side we were on.

We learned the words to rebel songs and read books about Easter 1916. Some of us joined underage Gaelic football teams in London. We were Irish wannabes, derided by Irish relations as 'Plastic Paddies' for not being the genuine article.

And London Irishness was different from Irish Irishness or American Irishness. Cousins in Dublin or Boston weren't surrounded by English people, and couldn't understand why it was difficult - even dangerous - for us to wear shamrocks on St. Patrick's Day.

For our parents' generation, the bombings made things even more complicated. Their accents immediately identified them as Irish in a city where Irish people were killing civilians. They were keen to show suspicious Londoners that the IRA didn't represent them, and missed few chances to denounce the bombings. Irish clubs across London banned IRA songs - modern and ancient - from their dances lest there be any doubt about their loyalties.

On weekdays my dad worked as a postman, and when one of his workmates had his fingers blown off by an IRA letter bomb we were scared he would be next. At weekends he moonlighted as a cabbie, and we waited in silence for his safe return every time a news flash interrupted evening television to report another random bombing in central London.

When we reached our late teens, most of my schoolmates and I were faced with the Great Passport Decision. Those of us with Irish parents had the choice to be British subjects or Irish citizens. It was an official, legal choice. You could be one or the other. Some opted for an Irish passport because it was a few pounds cheaper, but for others it was a decision loaded with political significance. The weekend of my 18th birthday, Bobby Sands began his hunger strike, and I chose an Irish passport.

The arrival of an Irish passport was the ultimate validation of our claims - there it was, in green and white, our national status legally declared. True, we had not been born in Ireland, but we had chosen Ireland in a way our Kerry cousins had never done, and surely that made us even more Irish?

A few years later, things became easier for London Irish teenagers. Random bombings in the city were rare, and while militant Republicanism still has its pull for some youngsters (Londoner Diarmuid O'Neill joined the IRA, and was shot dead by police in Hammersmith in 1996), modern Irish London offers more than a miserable anti-Englishness.

The success of The Pogues helped legitimise being Irish in London, and even made it trendy, while soccer stars like Tony Cascarino and Andy Townsend replaced Mac Stiofain (Chief of Staff of the Provisional IRA in 1970) as the new Cockney Irish heroes. Today's London kids with Irish parents are free from the edginess of the 1970s, and now the Irish or English dilemma is far more likely to be argued in the context of sport or music than political violence.

Many years ago I left London, and went to live in Ireland, more at home than I ever felt in my life. Living in Ireland was all I hoped it would be when I dreamt of it 25 years ago. I played soccer in the local sports club where I was known, inevitable, as 'the English fella'. I have since returned to England.

This book aims to help define what it means to be second or third generation Irish today. It traces the history of prominent and unsung second/third generation individuals in the founding of the modern Irish state, and examines how the recent Troubles have helped shape modern second/third generation Irish identity in Britain.

There is significant academic research currently under way into recent second and third generation Irish experience in Britain, and this book does not pretend to compete with the breadth or depth of those studies. It is instead a modest attempt to help fill some of the gaps in knowledge about the contribution of second/third generation Irish people to the fight for Irish independence, and how some people responded to growing up second generation Irish in Britain during the Troubles.

1.

Irish like Mick McCarthy and Morrissey

It's not clear who invented the term Plastic Paddy, or when it was first used. According to one academic report, it came into 'quite common use in the 1980s, frequently articulated by new middle-class Irish migrants in Britain, for whom it was a means of distancing themselves from established Irish communities'.[1]

It is an abusive term used by British and Irish people to ridicule the identity of second and third generation Irish people in Britain, and cheerfully ignores the historical record of Irish people born outside Ireland who have played key roles in Irish history. The idea is, of course, that unless you were born in Ireland you can't be properly Irish, and to claim that you are is somehow fraudulent.

But being socially ridiculed as a Plastic Paddy today is far less serious than the experiences some second and third generation Irish people had to endure during the Troubles. In the 1970s particularly, being identified as Irish could mean being arrested, interrogated or falsely convicted of terrorist offences.

It's not clear either how many second generation Irish people there were in Britain during the Troubles. Educated estimates put the figure of people born in Britain with at least one Irish-born parent at about 1.7 million. Surveys suggest that most second generation Irish people come from families with an Irish-born father and a non-Irish – probably English – mother.[2]

Census figures compiled in 2001 do not make the picture very much clearer. They suggest only 642,000 Irish people were living in England and Wales in that year. Despite a campaign by Irish groups to encourage second and third generation Irish people to tick the new ethnic minority box marked 'Irish', far fewer than expected did so. Perplexingly, almost 700,000 people put their place of birth as Ireland yet 53,000 fewer ticked the box identifying themselves as Irish. The 2001 census was the first time an Irish ethnic minority tickbox was offered, and there may have been some confusion about whether it was appropriate to mark it, especially from Irish people born in Britain.[3]

A substantial study called the *Irish 2 Project* aims to fill the gap in knowledge on second generation identity, and undertook wide research into the opinions and values of second generation Irish people living in Britain. 'One of our main findings,' said the authors, 'is that children of Irish migrants find it difficult to claim an Irish identity, even when they feel strongly Irish – their Irishness is denied by Irish and British people alike'.[4]

What we do know is that second generation Irish people generally have higher educational levels than their British counterparts, and that being second generation Irish is almost certainly bad for your health. A series of studies has indicated that second generation Irish people in Britain have significantly higher mortality rates than their English and Welsh counterparts. Research from 1996 shows that mortality rates for second generation Irish men and women of working age (15-64 for men and 15-59 for women) was significantly higher than for other groups in Britain.[5]

Even when social class differences were taken into account in a 1997 study, the mortality rates appear inexplicably high for second generation Irish people. Whereas the mortality rate for all men in semi- and unskilled work was 19 per cent higher than average, for second generation Irish it was 48 per cent higher. The mortality rates of second generation Irish men and women aged 15-44 was higher by more than 40 per cent compared to overall rates in England and Wales.[6]

A UK Office of National Statistics report in February 1999 showed, compared to the average figures for England and Wales, second generation Irish women suffer 60 per cent more lung, ovarian and cervical cancers, and men suffer 50 per cent more prostate cancer. Death rates among original Irish migrants and their children were also higher than for those who remained in Ireland. Statisticians conceded that, even taking into account socio-economic factors, the much higher cancer rates were 'a mystery'. 'Poor health may be the result of the persisting effect of parental socio-economic disadvantage and these studies demonstrate that health differences may not disappear rapidly following migration and can persist across several generations,' noted report author Seeromanie Harding.[7]

While the reasons for such poor health remain unclear, some researchers have suggested it might be linked to political and religious differences that have led to disadvantages for second generation Irish people in England and Wales, or even that anti-Irish and anti-Catholic attitudes may have somehow impacted on this group's health and sense of identity, although so far the evidence for these claims is thin. We know too that there was a demographic 'bulge' of children born in Britain in the late 1950s and early 1960s to Irish parents. These children's formative teenage years coincided with the earliest, most violent years of the Troubles.[8]

Several sustained IRA bombing campaigns in England forcefully shaped second and third generation Irish people's sense of identity. Some were so influenced by what was happening in Northern Ireland that they joined one of the paramilitary organisations there, or signed up for the British Army. Others were arrested and detained under the *Prevention of Terrorism Act* (PTA), and some found themselves victims of miscarriages of justice.

When the police raided the home of the Maguires, an Irish family living in Harlesdon, north London, on December 3, 1974, they were looking for explosives in connection with IRA bombs that had killed five people in a Guildford pub two months before. The police made several arrests and took the family to the police station to have their hands tested for traces of bomb-making activity.

The London-born children were included in the roundup and as they were being taken to the police station their mother, Anne Maguire, pleaded: 'Don't touch them. They're English'. A little while later at the station, 13 year-old Patrick Maguire told Detective Sergeant Hunt he thought the police were at his house 'because we're Irish, I suppose'. The raid eventually resulted in the wrongful conviction of seven people in the house that evening, including Patrick and his 16 year-old London-born brother Vincent.[9]

The wrongful convictions were part of a wider pattern, with four more people wrongly convicted of the IRA bombs at Guildford, and six more wrong convictions for the IRA bombing of Birmingham pubs.

Judith Ward was wrongly convicted of the M62 coach bombing of February 1974, when nine soldiers, two women and one child were killed by a bomb left in a bus carrying British soldiers from Manchester to Catterick. Ward apparently confessed to all sorts of IRA activity, including explosions at Euston station the previous September. It emerged that Ward had a mental disorder, her confessions were fanciful concoctions and the forensic evidence against her was false. In fact, the Court of Appeal accused the forensic scientists involved of having 'taken the law into their own hands'. Her conviction was quashed in June 1992.[10]

Ward was English and spun an elaborate series of tales to convince the security forces she was involved at a high level in the IRA. She falsely insisted she had married IRA figure Michael McVerry, and that she herself was a high-level operative. She was not second generation Irish, but to substantiate her fantastic stories she repeatedly claimed that she was.[11] In March 1972 she told the police her parents were from Cork. Four months later she was questioned in Belfast by British Army Sergeant Reynard of the Royal Electrical and Mechanical Engineers, and told him her parents were from Dublin. In February 1974 she was interrogated by police Sergeant Giltrap at police headquarters in Liverpool, and told him her father was born in Offaly (in fact he had been born in Stockport in 1925). Ward's confessions claimed a false second generation status to make her appear a more likely republican paramilitary.[12]

For many real second generation Irish people the Troubles were not the defining element in their lives, but an added complication to the difficult question of national and cultural identity. Did, and does, being second generation Irish make you Irish, English, both, or properly neither? It is not an exclusively modern dilemma. Born in Liverpool in 1901, Timothy O'Mara grew up in the city grappling with a conundrum familiar to many second and third generation Irish people. He wrote in his memoirs, first published in 1933:

> What I derived from my elementary English-Irish schooling was an intense love for the British Empire and an equally intense hatred for England as opposed to Ireland. Our mothers and fathers, of course, were unequivocal in their attitude – destroy England, no less! But we children... were rather patronized and Britishized... The paradox has remained in my makeup for years. The sound of a patriotic air will make me want to get out my shillelagh for the old wrongs of Ireland; but the moment the music is over, common sense will warn me to put it back.[13]

And contemporary poet Tom Paulin, born in Leeds and brought up in Belfast, says: 'I feel bits and pieces... I do feel more Irish than anything else'. Nowadays, with the Troubles assumed to be over in most practical senses, the issue of second generation identity is far less vexed than it was 20 or 30 years ago.[14]

Second generation Irish journalist Joe Horgan only finds space in modern Britain to openly celebrate his identity on St Patrick's Day. 'On St. Patrick's Day we are visible. For the rest of the year the Irish in Britain, especially the second generation Irish, just disappear into the rest of the community,' he said.

> We have white faces, British accents, local lives. We are secretly Irish. But on Paddy's Day we come out of the closet. Get it all off our chests. We come clean. No more skulking around. No more secret smirking when England lose at cricket, football, tennis or whatever game they strangely believe they should be world champions in. No more uncomfortable shifting in our seats when they talk about 'us' and you know inside you're not them. No more discomfort in having a mental geography that is as much Cork, Donegal, Galway as it is Birmingham, Manchester, London.[15]

Indeed, these days claiming Irish identity is sometimes considered hip, conferring instant credibility and cachet. Paul Farrelly, MP for Newcastle-under-Lyme declared proudly 'I can safely say that I am the only new Labour member of parliament to be the grandson of a rabbit trapper from County Meath'.[16]

In 1965, Shay Brennan became the first English-born player to play for Ireland, after a change in the eligibility rules of the Fédération Internationale de Football Association (FIFA). Sixteen of the 22-man Irish squad for the World Cup in Italy in 1990 were born outside Ireland. Star Irish players like Andy Townsend and John Aldridge had never stepped foot in Ireland before arriving to make their debuts. Current mid-fielder Stephen Reid even played at under-16 level for England before opting to play for Ireland.

'I remember as a kid asking my dad whether I was English or Irish,' said former Irish soccer captain and manager Mick McCarthy. 'It wasn't about football – I wasn't that arrogant that I thought I was going to play for England or Ireland – it was just a question of my nationality. He said I could play for either, I had dual nationality, which was kind of cool when I was a kid. It wasn't something my mates had.'[17]

McCarthy's decision to send captain Roy Keane home from the Irish World Cup training camp in May 2002 triggered uproar in Ireland, with the bust-up dominating Irish news media coverage for over a week. The fall-out centred on Keane's outburst at McCarthy during a meeting called by the manager. What made Keane's tirade white-hot for many were early reports that Keane, in the midst of an abusive onslaught, had questioned McCarthy's Irishness. Dublin's *Evening Herald* trumpeted 'What Keane said to McCarthy' on May 24, and printed on the front page a purportedly verbatim account of Keane's verbal assault.

> Who the f**k do you think you are having meetings about me? You were a crap player and you are a crap manager. The only reason I have any dealings with you is that somehow you are the manager of my country and you're not even Irish, you English c***[18]

What shocked many was not the swearing – anyone who has spent time in soccer dressing rooms will know it is far from unusual – but the reference to McCarthy's Englishness. *Irish Times* sportswriter Tom Humphries explained three days later: 'Once Roy raised the issue of Irishness there was no turning back, there was no quick band-aid that would fit neatly over the wound. He opened up a fissure that should never have been explored.' Humphries (who was born in London and spent his early years there) noted that eleven of the Irish squad, like McCarthy, spoke with English accents.

> Keane had prised open a subject which is never spoken about, never alluded to. Brian Kerr's youth teams often play practice games whereby culchies play the Dubs [countrysiders versus Dubliners] and those with English accents play on the side their parents came from. It's a nice way of dividing the players for a little fun and it integrates everyone. You could live in London all your

> life and not know that deep down you are a culchie. No Irish youth or senior team though would ever divide itself up along the lines of English accents and Irish accents. Too sensitive. Too wrong.[19]

In the fallout during the following weeks, Keane (whose wife and children are second generation Irish) denied questioning McCarthy's nationality. But whether founded in rumour or fact the issue was uncomfortably alive in the media for several days.

Ireland striker Niall Quinn was in the room during the attack on McCarthy, and recognised how delicate the issue was. 'There's the "English cunt" business,' he said.

> Somebody has decided that this was one of the phrases that Roy threw at Mick. It wasn't, but it's a sensitive area to start digging into. Players raised as Irish people in England were in the room that night and they know it wasn't said, but reading it now as fact they must wonder is 'English' a key part of the insult? If Mick McCarthy can be regarded as 'English', what about me? Are we all the same here or are we not?[20]

In many ways, the issue is one of accent rather than birth. Former Irish soccer star Paul McGrath was born in Ealing and moved to Dublin when he was six weeks old, and David O'Leary was born in Islington and moved to Dublin as a toddler. Neither are considered as anything other than Irish, whereas current full back Steve Finnan was born in Limerick but moved to London as a child and has a Cockney accent.

For second and third generation Irish musicians in the 1970s, 1980s and 1990s, the issue of their identity, and their attitude to Northern Ireland, produced a variety of responses. In 1972, John Lennon and Paul McCartney both reacted with protest songs after Bloody Sunday, when 13 unarmed civilians were shot dead by British soldiers in Derry.

Lennon's grandfather Jack was born in Dublin, but spent most of his life in the US as a professional singer (he was an original member of the Kentucky Minstrels). Although John Winston

Lennon was named in tribute to IRA nemesis Churchill, he had been publicly identified with the IRA as early as August 1971, when he and Yoko Ono joined a political demonstration in London. They walked up Oxford St with 1500 marchers opposing British policy on Northern Ireland, and he carried a placard reading 'For the IRA, Against British Imperialism'.[21]

Lennon and Yoko Ono's song *Sunday Bloody Sunday* identifies with an angry Irish perspective:

> When Stormont bans our marches they've got a lot to learn.
> Internment is no answer, it's those mothers' turn to burn!...
> You anglo pigs and Scotties sent to colonise the North
> You wave your bloody Union Jack and you know what it's worth!

Lennon's *Luck of the Irish* song refers to learning about Irish history in Liverpool, and is similarly angry:

> In the 'Pool they told us the story
> How the English divided the land...
> Blame it all on the kids, the IRA
> As the bastards commit genocide![22]

Lennon sang and spoke at a protest meeting outside the New York offices of British airline BOAC the week after Bloody Sunday. About 5,000 people attended the protest and he and Yoko sang *Luck of the Irish*, the proceeds of which they announced would go to the civil rights movement in Northern Ireland. Lennon made a short speech before the song about his Irish ancestry. 'My name is Lennon and you can guess the rest,' he told the crowd. He said he'd been brought up in Liverpool, which, he claimed, was 80 per cent dominated by Irish descent, and told the crowd that in England Liverpool was known as 'the capital of Ireland'.[23]

Ellen Duncan, a New York-based activist for Irish civil rights, went to see John and Yoko two days later. 'A lot of the conversation was about him being Irish from Liverpool and how he identified [with the minority community in Northern Ireland]', she said. They talked about the tragedy of Bloody Sunday and, she said, he alluded to his sense of split identity. 'Him being English felt very responsible to do something and being Irish Liverpudlian… he felt a kind of responsibility.'[24]

But Yoko's friend, radical feminist Kate Millet, derided Lennon's involvement in Irish issues. 'He must have felt a certain foolishness,' she said. 'Liverpool Irish, what's that?' she scoffed.[25]

Although Paul McCartney had Irish grandparents on both sides of his family, he had no hesitation in identifying himself as anything but English. His hit *Give Ireland Back to the Irish* was written in immediate response to Bloody Sunday. It went to number one in Ireland (and Spain) but was immediately banned by the BBC for its political content. The song is written from an English person's perspective of injustice to 'them' – rather than 'us' – Irish. He explained:

> … when the English paratroopers, my army who I'm payin' rates for, go into Ireland and shoot down innocent bystanders, for the first time in my life I go, Hey, wait a minute, we're the goodies, aren't we? That wasn't very goody. And I'm moved to make some kind of a protest.[26]

Some second generation Irish kids growing up during the Troubles managed to carve out successful careers as music writers and performers without referring much to their thoughts on Northern Ireland. Irish identity does not appear as an obvious theme for second generation songwriters like Billy Idol, Boy George or Kate Bush (although Bush's 1978 debut number one single *Wuthering Heights* was a tribute to second generation Irish writer Emily Bronte).

For others, like Wolverhampton-born Kevin Rowland of Dexy's Midnight Runners, a second generation status proved more obviously inspirational. His self-styled 'Celtic soul' sound produced the smash 1982 hit *Come on Eileen*, a number one in the UK and the US (which urged us to 'Sing just like our fathers…')

and a series of other critically acclaimed pieces like *Dance Stance*, a pointedly political song about anti-Irish racism:

> How about Oscar Wilde and Brendan Behan?
> Talking about Sean O'Casey, Edna O'Brien.
> Shut it, you don't understand it.
> Shut your mouth til you know the truth.

While little of The Smiths' work appears to refer to the Troubles or their second generation experience, songwriter and lead singer Morrissey insists that it played a huge part in his – and the band's – development.

> With so much Irishness around us, my sister and I growing up, never really felt we were Mancunians. My Irishness was never something I hid or camouflaged. I grew up in a strong Irish community. Of course, early on I'd be teased about it, I was called 'Paddy' from an early age. I mean, there I was, born, raised and bred in Manchester but I was still always called 'Paddy'... It steeped into everything I knew growing up. I was very aware of being Irish and we were told that we were quite separate from the scruffy kids around us – we were different to them... It was always odd later on with The Smiths when I was described as being 'extremely English' because other people would tell me that I looked Irish, I sounded Irish and had other tell-tale signs.
>
> In fact, the new album – which I have finished writing but has yet to be recorded – is called *Irish Blood, English Heart*. It's funny, because U2 are always portrayed as being famously Irish and this is the great unsaid: aren't half the band English? [Dave 'The Edge' Evans was born in Barking, Essex, and Adam Clayton was born in Oxfordshire.] All you have to do is hear The Smiths' surnames – Maher, Morrissey, Joyce and Rourke. It was only actually Andy Rourke's mother who was an English parent – all the other parents were Irish.[27]

Irish blood, English Heart includes the lyrics: 'This I'm made of / There is no-one I'm afraid of…'

Noel and Liam Gallagher are also second generation Irish musicians from Manchester. The original line-up of their band Oasis was made up of five second generation Irish boys. Noel Gallagher said 'Manchester was just a great place to be – everyone I knew was second generation Irish.' Yet the Troubles have yet to feature as a theme in the Gallaghers' work. Noel 'talks of Mother Ireland as "where I grew up,"' noted one journalist. 'Somebody asked him the other day whether he was patriotic. How can I be? he replied. "Because I am as Irish as I am English, and that makes me cooler than you are for a f***ing start."'[28]

The Gallaghers' father Tommy, from Meath, started an underage Gaelic football team in Manchester, and Noel can apparently recall scoring a point at Croke Park during a schoolboy tournament for an under 14s team. As a child, he says he listened to 'All the Dubliners and the Chieftains and the Wolfe Tones. We were brought up listening to that stuff and all the country and western stuff as well'.[29]

Despite the hard rock star image, Noel and his brother Liam conform to many second generation traditions. Liam Gallagher's children were baptised in the faith of their Irish family. 'My mam and all my aunties are still Catholics. Music's my stuff… My kids'll go to Catholic school and be brought up that way and if one of 'em wants to be a priest, fucking fair play and if one of them wants to be a rock star, then fine.'(One of the potential priests is called Lennon, in tribute to Liam's hero John.)[30]

In contrast, while Elvis Costello (born Declan Patrick McManus in London) downplays Irish cultural influence on his music he has written several songs about British-Irish conflict. His 1981 hit *Oliver's Army* is about British Army occupation of Northern Ireland ('It's no laughing party when you've been on the murder mile/Only takes one itchy trigger, one more widow, one less white nigger') but he is far from eager to claim an Irish identity.

> I don't think I have an anything identity, I'm just me. I've spent a lot of time in Ireland, I like it…, but I don't think

> there can be anything more nauseating than a cod-anything. I do notice that I tend to be Irish in the eyes of the press when it suits them now... Obviously there's some sort of connection there in the blood but the problem is it's kind of green beer territory... there's problems with wholly identifying with a culture, where you just go blindly into accepting that all things Irish are great. You usually find the worst offenders of that are the ex-pats or the 4th generation people. Whether it be politics or culture or anything, they're the ones that are blindly, uncritically Irish...[31]

His *Any King's Shilling* song from the 1989 *Spike* album tells of an Irish man warning an Irish member of the British army not to put on his uniform in an attempt to save his life.

> 'Stay at home tonight if you know what's good for you.
> I can't say more it would be telling
> For if you don't what will become of you
> Just isn't worth any king's shilling.
> Please don't put your silly head in that British soldier's hat

> It's a true story. It's something that happened here in Dublin to my grandfather, or so he told. He was orphaned in Birkenhead and he ended up in an orphanage in the south of England, and after he left that he was put in the army... he was sent to France [during the First World War] and he was wounded, badly wounded... he was out from fighting and was stationed in Dublin... he told that story as actually happening to him while he was here. He was from a completely Irish community in Birkenhead and he probably saw nothing unusual in having lots of Irish friends and they said to him, 'Listen, you better watch out...'

Costello's grandparents on his father's side were Irish emigrees 'from God knows where'. Although the Irish connections were 'close enough to have a strong influence on my father', Elvis said he 'grew to really dislike folk music because the attitude of a lot of the folkies was so prejudiced against anything original'. Then he saw The Pogues. Costello produced The Pogues' second album and had to 'drag back all these things that I had filed in the back of my head about this music'.

The Pogues also wrote and performed unashamedly political songs, including a call for the release of the Guildford Four and the Birmingham Six in their 1986 song *Streets of Sorrow/Birmingham Six*. The Pogues became iconic figures for the younger Irish diaspora in the 1980s and 1990s, their attraction partly centred on their own second generation identities and song titles like *Lullaby of London*, *Misty Morning*, *Albert Bridge* and *Fairytale of New York* were richly evocative of Irish exile experience.

Phil Chevron of the Pogues explained:

> The Pogues could never have been an Irish band indigenously – it could never have happened in Ireland. It would never have happened from within the island. The Pogues needed to happen from the diaspora… there are two Irelands – the people who live on the island and there's the people who went away or who are second generation and very often that gives us a different point of view on the culture and what it is to be Irish.

In fact, only two of the nine Pogues featured on the band's website are listed as born in Ireland. The Pogues represented a new, harder-edged Irish diaspora. 'The only politics that counted for anything on the London-Irish scene were being Irish in a place that was innately racist towards the Irish,' said Chevron.[32]

The band was fronted by legendary songwriter and lead singer Shane MacGowan. 'One of the things that Shane's early work spoke for was this huge group of people that were second generation Irish,' said Chevron. 'Shane gave them a voice – we had been used to cowering in corners pretending not to be Irish or subliminating that completely, and Shane was the first person to stand up and not be embarrassed about it and shout about it.'[33]

The Pogues emerged from the London punk scene of the late 70s, and MacGowan explained his early musical influence included the second generation Irish punk legend Johnny Rotten. 'I wouldn't have been that interested in them (the Sex Pistols) if Johnny Rotten hadn't been so bloody obviously Irish and made such a big noise about it and made such anti-English records,' he said.[34]

Johnny Rotten was born and brought up John Lydon in north London '...but every year we'd go to Ireland, where my father and mother were born, for six- or eight-week holidays... My Irish half provided my sense of devilry,' he said. Lydon struggled to find full acceptance in Ireland and London.'[My grandfather]... was famous for being in the Irish independent army (sic)... He hated the English and probably hated me and my brother Jimmy. We spoke with thick Cockney accents that he could not stand.' Back in London, his identity did not fit in either. 'When I was very young and going to school, I remember bricks thrown at me by English parents. [They'd shout] "Those dirty Irish bastards!", that kind of shit... We were the Irish scum.'[35]

Lydon's parents' refusal to teach him Gaelic 'left me isolated and shallow inside. I wanted to go out of my way and find out about my own Irishness, but when I did get there, it was never as romantic as books made it out to be,' he recalled.[36]

Lydon's teenage friend Billy Idol achieved music fame with punk band Generation X and as a solo artist. He also found growing up second generation Irish in north London in the 1970s difficult.

> My mother came from Cork, just like John's mum. When I was a little boy we'd go to Ireland at least once a year to see her family. They used to call me the British kid because I had such an English accent. It seemed like everywhere I went, I was the outcast. When my mother used to watch something about Ireland on TV she'd say 'I hate the British'.[37]

Lydon says his early punk days were a reaction against the conventionality of music in the mid-70s, when everything was 'So English'. Yet his anger, and sense of Irish identity, did not express itself in support for Irish republicanism.

> Things like gun running usually occur with Irish priests who are going back and forth between England and

> Ireland. You see them running round the Irish centres, collecting for 'our friends up North'... You can't allow yourself to get involved in that crap. Whatever those people are doing up there is not for the reasons they're pretending. It's like two mafia gangs punching each other out – UDA/IRA, IRA/UDA. They both run their extortion rackets and plague people no end.[38]

Lydon remembers seeing the young MacGowan at early Sex Pistols gigs.

> [He] used to come and see us play all the time. He'd be down in the front totally pissed out of his head in his Union Jack T-shirt. When he joined the Pogues, he traded it in for a tricolour. So funny. Just like that – instant nationality swap.[39]

MacGowan's birthplace is difficult to determine. Several accounts of his life mistakenly report that he was born in Ireland. No definitive answer is offered in his autobiography *A Drink With Shane MacGowan*, although the jacket blurb declares unequivocally he was 'born on a small farm in Tipperary', and according to a BBC documentary, *The Great Hunger*, MacGowan 'was born on the banks of the Shannon in rural Ireland'. In 1998 *The Irish Post* newspaper announced the singer was voted 70th most influential Irish person of all time, and that he was 'born in Tipperary'.[40]

In fact the public register confirms that Shane P.L. MacGowan was born in Tonbridge, Kent in England on Christmas Day, 1957. Within months of his birth, his family returned to Tipperary where Shane spent his early childhood, which appears to be enough for MacGowan to reject his second generation status. 'I'm first-generation Irish... Tipperary is my home,' he insisted in 1998. Quite why MacGowan, a hero of so many second generation Irish from Chicago to Cricklewood, is keen to deny he is one of them is unclear. Mystifyingly, the www.pogues.com website in March 2004 listed MacGowan's birthplace as Kent, Ireland.[41]

In fairness to second and third generation songwriters, there is no suggestion that they were deliberately avoiding issues by not writing about the Troubles. Very little produced by The Undertones, a young punk band in Derry during the late 1970s and early 1980s, refers to the daily reality of the violence around them. Asked why, guitar player John O'Neil explained:

> It's funny but the political thing never even crossed our minds at the time. Music was an escape. I was definitely wrapped up in the whole rock 'n' roll thing... talking about what went on in the North seemed... for old people.[42]

The late Paul Cunniffe was a significant figure on the Irish music scene in Britain and Ireland in the 1990s. Born in Britain in 1961, he moved to Ireland aged 14. He wrote the Saw Doctors' hit song *I Useta Love Her*, and was acutely conscious of the difficulties of being Irish in Ireland with an English accent. 'He loved Ireland... but he just felt he didn't fit in anywhere. It was a huge culture shock for him when he moved back to Galway,' said his partner Jo Hardy. 'His five younger brothers and sisters were alright – they soon developed local accents, but Paul was stuck with his east London accent.' The title track of his album is *Excuse My Accent*, which includes the lyrics:

> Excuse my accent, it's just the way I am.
> I talk like that, a very mixed up man.
> Children laugh behind my back because I talk like that..[43]

2.
Identity Parade

Young republicans detained without trial in the early 1970s looked to second generation Irish writer and comedian Spike Milligan to lift their spirits. Milligan was born in 1918 to Irish parents in India. His father, who was from Sligo, was a serving British soldier. Young Milligan was educated at convent schools before moving to London at the age of 16 when his father retired from the army.

'One of the books most passed around during internment was Spike Milligan's *Puckoon* which, I was assured when it was given to me, was about Crossmaglen and the Brits,' recalled senior republican Danny Morrison. 'Only later did I discover that it was published in 1960, was about a "partitioned" village (set in Sligo, I think) and was written before Milligan even set foot in Ireland.'

> Our love of Milligan was simplistic: he was an iconoclast of the British establishment and boasted of his Irish heritage at a time when many other Irish-born comics were anxious for promotional reasons to emphasise how Brit-friendly they were…[1]

Another second generation Irish comedian, Kevin Day, grew up in Streatham, South London, in the 1970s with an Irish mother and English father. 'There was a time when I was 15 or 16… all the voices I heard were Irish apart from my dad,' he said.

> I regularly went to Ireland, everything was focused on Ireland. School was very Irish. 95 per cent of the kids were from Irish backgrounds, and many of the teachers were pro-Irish and anti-English and so I went through a reaction against that. For a couple of years I firmly denied any Irishness. I wouldn't go to Ireland and stayed at home. I just didn't like it. I don't know now quite why I was so annoyed but I felt I was being fitted into the wrong box. I wasn't Irish. I didn't understand why there was so much emphasis on Ireland. When I went to Ireland I didn't feel part of the family. I struggled to make myself understood – I couldn't understand them, they couldn't understand me. I didn't feel accepted. I felt a stranger in Ireland and yet I felt I was being forced to accept that as something I liked. I didn't enjoy Ireland that much. My mum's from a massive family – she's got nine brothers and sisters and when I went over there I'd be forced into one of these houses with – as far as I was concerned – ten strangers who couldn't speak properly.[2]

Day briefly dallied with the far right in the late 1970s, and for a while became involved with the National Front.

> The flirtation with the far right was very much part of looking for an identity and was a reaction against the Irish thing. It was me looking for Britishness and an identity other than an Irish identity… I recall very little conversation about Ireland at any National Front meeting. It was purely focused on coloured immigrants. I think that was because there were quite a few people of Irish background in the National Front at that time.

The National Front phase ended after only about six months, when he was talked out of it by two classmates. Later, in his early 20s, he became involved with the politics of the far left. Then he

> decided the Irish identity was a good thing, and I'd go to the Swan in Stockwell every weekend and stand for the [Irish] national anthem because that gave me an identity

> in leftwing politics. I became aware of the causes of the Troubles and that became a handy cause for me and I grabbed the Irishness with both hands and I really did consider myself Irish for a time. I was really into the culture, even so far as to try to teach myself Gaelic. Then I realised my identity was really in London more than a nationality thing.

Day says his Irish background means he can perform material onstage that he wouldn't otherwise be able to do, but

> because of my [London] accent the problem is that you have to set up your Irish credentials before you do [the piece]. I find that you have to do that especially for the Irish people in the audience rather than the English people… because most English people would think it perfectly reasonable for me to comment on Ireland but there is the "what's it got to do with you" or "how dare you" [reaction from Irish people]. You need to let the audience know you're coming from [an Irish] perspective so you have to drop a line in… it reassures them you have a certain knowledge.

For instance, when performing in Belfast, Day explained how

> You have to say it's great to be here because I'm from just up the road, blahdy blahdy blah and gradually they'd take that on board and accept it but you can sense the frisson because they know, and in a sense you know, that whatever you consider your credentials to be you ain't living it and they really are… I did three nights there and by the third night I was doing appreciably less about Ireland.

Day based part of his act on a true story about Belfast zoo.

> There was a tiger recently escaped from the zoo and I used to do this routine about the tiger because it walked round Belfast for a few hours and then went back to its cage and there was this whole thing about it being black and orange in Belfast. And I used to do this thing about

> the marching season which was clearly anti the marches and about the fact that Ian Paisley was also chairman of Ulster Against Sodomy, and I used to do a thing about that… In an Irish audience, if they hear someone with an accent like mine doing material about Ireland, for some reason loyalists will hear it as anti-loyalist and republicans will hear it as anti-republican – they don't listen to the words.
>
> The only people who really challenge me about Irish stuff are squaddies or relatives of squaddies. I remember doing a piece when the IRA sent mortars into the garden of 10 Downing Street, and I was doing something essentially about the reaction of the politicians… you're not saying you advocate all-out war in Northern Ireland, but that's what they hear… Because I wasn't actively saying it [the attack] was a bad thing, and because I was getting laughs out of it people would come up afterwards and say 'My brother's out in Northern Ireland; do you want him to be killed?' and I'd say 'no', and 'You're not listening to the stuff I did anyway, and as it happens I don't think your brother should be in Northern Ireland'.

Other second generation Irish writers have also devoted considerable energy to analysing the situation in Northern Ireland in the context of their own identity. Margaretta D'Arcy was born in London of a Russian mother and Irish father and in the early 1970s spent two years as a member of Official Sinn Féin. In 1978 she was sent to Armagh Gaol for three weeks after she protested about an H-Block march being banned.

The following March she and eleven other women were arrested outside Armagh Gaol on International Woman's Day for protesting about the inhumane conditions in which women republicans were imprisoned. D'Arcy refused to pay her fine and in May 1980 was imprisoned for three months in Armagh Gaol where she joined republican women in their no-wash protests for political status. Her book, *Tell Them Everything*, details her experiences inside the prison.

Tony Geraghty, a former British paratrooper, was the *Sunday Times* correspondent in Northern Ireland in the late '60s and early '70s. Author of the SAS history *Who Dares Wins*, Geraghty was born in Liverpool and his mother, from Dublin, 'limped from a bullet wound in the ankle collected in an earlier phase of the Irish struggle,' he claimed.[3]

Geraghty said any instinctive sympathy he had for the republican cause disappeared with Bloody Friday, when the IRA killed nine civilians in a series of car bombs on one day in July 1972. 'This was the moment when my sympathy for the nationalist cause in the Province – explicit enough to have earned a few beatings, one by the RUC at Stormont, as well as a reputation among Conservative ministers as "that republican reporter" – underwent a radical rethink,' he said.[4]

By the time his book *The Irish War: The Military History of a Domestic Conflict* appeared in 1998, he had little enthusiasm for any Irish nationalism, and derided the Birmingham-born republican Phelim Ó Hadmaill as 'a reconstructed expatriate Irishman in search of his roots… a stock figure on the landscape of this war…'[5]

London-Irish journalist Martin McNamara started covering Northern Ireland issues in the mid-'80s, and found that his second generation identity meant 'lots of people expected me to take a very particular stance on the Northern Ireland conflict and I wasn't interested in doing that; almost perversely I was determined to play it straight down the middle'. In 1987 he interviewed UDA leader John McMichael in Belfast, shortly before McMichael was assassinated.

> Going to the UDA headquarters was frightening for several different reasons. One, it was almost my first interview, so I was feeling very nervous. Then there is the Catholic thing. I got the strong feeling in Belfast that people were checking out your name and knew from it your religion. I went up to the heavily fortified door, under the cctv and anti-bomb netting, and said who I was

> over the tannoy. This old woman repeated my name with some sort of astonishment. She wasn't much happier when she let me in and led us to a room, past lots of vaguely rude Private Eye-style pictures of the Pope with slogans about Popery.[6]

Kevin Toolis' excellent analysis of the Troubles is written from a self consciously second generation perspective. *Rebel Hearts – Journeys Within the IRA's Soul* charts his exploration for the roots of modern-day republicanism from the starting point of his Edinburgh birth and upbringing. Toolis went to the same school as James Connolly, and suggests his life would have been very different had he been first and not second generation Irish. 'My brothers fought for better exam results, not Irish freedom. Instead of prison I went to Edinburgh University… But that was an accident of history. I could so easily have joined the IRA.'[7]

Toolis' impressive perspective on the Troubles, and the place of a second generation republican in them, finally concludes that, for him, the differences between first and second generation are too wide to bridge. 'I cannot say I am truly an Irish republican; I lack the intensity for it, I would not kill for it….'[8]

Of course, there are as many second generation Irish experiences and definitions of identity as there are second generation people. John Walsh and I grew up in Battersea, south London, during the 1960s and 1970s within a mile of each other, at roughly the same time. But John Walsh's upbringing as described in the elegantly-written 1999 book *Falling Angels* is a world away from my experience. His parents went to posh dinners and dances at the Irish club in Eaton Square, and existed in a different Irish London to mine. Walsh's father was our family doctor when I was a boy. I was friends with his cleaner's son, but socially our families' paths would never have intersected. His London Irish upbringing was an oddly solitary one.

He went to a school where he was the only kid with Irish parents – had he gone to the local Catholic school where I went he would have been surrounded by Irish names and customs. He missed out too on playing GAA or going to Irish pubs and clubs where he would have met many other London Irish kids grappling with their identity.

Walsh perceptively outlines the common dilemmas of second generation Irish.

> I'm used to Irish ways and behaviour, the drift of conversation and friendship… [yet] every time I open my mouth, I'm reminded how much I don't fit in with this Hibernian gang, how little I share their mind-set, their sympathies, their prejudices, their devotion to strange gods and crackpot mythologies.

He eventually resolves the conflict inside him by plumping for Englishness, and emphatically describes himself as 'I, who am not Irish'.[9]

Second generation Irish writer Pete McCarthy embarked on a similar quest for the answer to his identity in the genuinely funny *McCarthy's Bar*.

> England leaves me feeling detached: an outsider, and observer, in some way passing through. But as soon as I hit the tarmac or the quayside over there, I feel involved, engaged – as if I've come home, even though I've never actually lived there. So what I'm wondering is this. Is it possible to have some kind of genetic memory of a place where you've never lived, but your ancestors have?[10]

Pushing the theme further, but without finding a solution, he concludes: 'I'm wondering whether it's possible to belong in a place where you weren't born and didn't grow up.'[11]

After years of soul-searching McCarthy concludes somewhat indecisively: 'I'm half and half [Irish/English] I think… Whether there is such a thing as genetic memory or whether I'm just a tragic Plastic Paddy who's been conned by the tourist board adverts and the Van Morrison albums and the Guinness ads I don't know but [Ireland] just works for me.'[12]

What is remarkable about both McCarthy's and Walsh's books is how little impact the Troubles in Northern Ireland appear to have had on their definitions of Irishness. Walsh, growing up in the very turbulent London of the early 1970s while the city was being regularly bombed by the IRA, resulting in all sorts of dislocation and trauma for the London-Irish community, breezes over the issue in a couple of pages, while McCarthy barely mentions it at all.

Even when allowance is made for a wide spectrum of second generation experiences, a brief scan of some second generation Irish characters in written fiction produces some genuinely absurd representations. In *Shake Hands With the Devil*, Rearden Conner's 1934 novel about earlier Troubles, Kerry Sutton is a north Londonder with an Irish mother and English father who arrives in Dublin in 1921 to study medicine and in three years also masters the Irish language. Although he possesses 'not the slightest interest in politics', an improbable coincidence leads to him being caught up in a skirmish with British soldiers, which forces him into the hands of the IRA.[13]

Before being sworn into the organisation, he is asked about his English background and told that because of it,

> you may be of valuable assistance to us. Psychology plays a great part in this situation. One of the finest of England's weapons is the natural phlegm of her people. It is almost impossible for us to discover how they'll react to one of our moves or just how they'll counter-move. On the other hand, you may find after the first flush of enthusiasm has worn off that your sympathy really lies with England. That, perhaps, would be natural after having lived there for such a long time. However, it would be disastrous for you.

He is offered dubious advice on how to lose any lingering English affiliation. 'Stamp it out of your mind as a monk stamps out sexual vision. You can't serve two masters, Sutton!'[14]

Sutton's untenable belief that 'both sides are right,' some love interest with a beautiful English hostage and a growing disdain for his IRA comrades ('Clodhoppers really! Why, they'd stare their eyes out if they saw an underground train!') leads him to defect to the British. 'His whole trouble,' it seems, 'was that the English strain in him was more powerful than the Irish.'[15]

Sutton leads the Black and Tans to his IRA unit, who are all wiped out. Then, because his affiliation can't be fully trusted, and because he's wearing a Fainne [Irish speaking] badge, the Tans kill him anyway.

Interestingly, in the film version of the book made in 1959 and starring Michael Redgrave, Cyril Cusack and James Cagney, Sutton's name is changed to Kerry O'Shea. In the film version, he fought for the Allies in France, and has an American, instead of an English, background. He is far more reluctant to join the IRA than his print counterpart even though (unlike Sutton) his father was a republican martyr.

David Lodge's 1962 novel *Ginger, You're Barmy*, is set in England during the 1950s and recounts the national service days of Jonathan Browne and his friend Mike 'Ginger' Brady, a second generation Irish lad who 'distinguished himself at university by speaking against birth control'. But Brady is drawn as an heroic, sensitive and physically strong figure, far from a two-dimensional Irish stereotype unsure about his identity.

> 'Are you Irish, Mike?…
> 'No, unfortunately. Otherwise I wouldn't be here [conscripted to the British Army]. My parents are Irish, but I was born in England.'[16]

Brady deserts from the British Army and joins the IRA, but is disillusioned fairly quickly. 'There's not much to choose between them [the IRA and British Army]' he confides to his friend. 'A few weeks ago the fools blew up a telephone booth in Armagh, and some people were hurt. That was enough for me. We made a deal, that if I helped them with this raid, they'd get me to South America.'[17] Brady's IRA career ends when he's sent to prison, making his father 'secretly proud,' while the narrator's verdict is that Brady 'was no hero, he was barmy, and there was no place for him'.[18]

Robin Moore's truly awful *Kaufman Snatch* of 1976 – littered with factual errors, absurd characters and typos – features

Commandant O'Rourke of the IRA. He discovers that his speech in Irish to comrades welcoming him out of prison is met with blank stares because 'born and bred in Liverpool' he spoke 'in accents unfamiliar to them'.[19]

In *The Good Terrorist*, Doris Lessing's Booker–shortlisted novel of 1985, a bourgeois revolutionary group in London unsuccessfully attempts to offer services to the IRA. Though laughably incompetent, the inept cell is vaguely connected to more serious figures – the shadowy Andrew Connors, who has an Irish father, and the third generation Irish Gordon O'Leary, who store and move weapons for the IRA.[20]

The devastatingly handsome Fr Paul O'Shaughnessey, a second generation Irish priest from New York, ends up talking to Padraig Pearse in Kilmainham Jail in Morgan Llywelyn's *1916* novel published in 1998. Pearse reads O'Shaughnessey a poem shortly before the republican leader is taken out for execution.[21]

Two of the characters in Jamie O'Neill's *At Swim, Two Boys*, published in 1997, are South African-born brothers, Gordie and Jim Mack. They are caught up in the turbulent politics of Irish independence in the early part of the twentieth century. Gordie, the elder, joins the Irish Volunteers, sides with Redmond and is killed fighting for the British Army in the First World War, while Jim fights with the Citizen Army in St. Stephen's Green during the 1916 Easter Rising, and later for the IRA during the Civil War.[22]

There were real second generation republicans fighting in St. Stephens's Green during Easter Week, though their contribution – and those of their British-born comrades elsewhere in Dublin that week – is often overlooked.

As a teenager, Ernie Nunan from Brixton in south London fought with his brother Sean in the GPO. As an old man more than 50 years later he was upset at aspersions cast on his motives, and those of his London colleagues, for joining the Rising, and wrote an article for *An t-Oglach*, the IRA newspaper, to put the record straight.

> A book called *Headquarters Battalion Easter Week 1916* says 'these men [from London, Liverpool and other

> British cities] had returned to Ireland to avoid being forced into the war on England's side'. This is far from the truth. They came to participate in the Rising.

Nunan says the Irish Volunteers in Britain 'consisted of men born in Ireland, and also of men born in England and Scotland, from 1st to 4th generations'.[23] He recounts that some weeks before the Rising the Liverpool unit of the Volunteers arrived in Dublin and set up camp in Kimmage to prepare for others coming from England, and 'thus became the first standing Army of the Irish Republic'.

The contribution of the Nunan brothers and the other second generation Irish to the Rising and the War for Independence is routinely ignored by historians, film-makers and novelists in their accounts of the period. In one of the most breathtakingly daring incidents of the war with Britain, IRA leader Michael Collins and Ernie Nunan's brother Sean were smuggled into police headquarters in Dublin's Brunswick Street one night in April 1919 where they risked their lives poring through the secret intelligence files the police had on the IRA.

Yet in eminent historian T. Ryle Dwyer's 1998 biography of Collins, Nunan is airbrushed out of the escapade – the clandestine raid on Brunswick Street is described at some length, but with Collins as the lone hero. Similarly, when the episode is portrayed as a key incident in the 1996 Neil Jordan film *Michael Collins*, there is no sign of Sean Nunan as the solitary Collins spends the night among the files unaided by the boy from Brixton.[24]

Perhaps it would have been too complicated to explain why a trusted accomplice of Collins had a south London accent, but whatever the reason, there is no room for Sean Nunan's bravery in the biopic. It has no room, either, for any but Irish accents in the scenes set in the GPO, despite the presence of plenty of other Londoners, Liverpudlians and Glaswegians fighting with the Nunans for the Volunteers. Similarly, in RTÉ's lavish historical drama in the year 2000, *Rebel Heart*, only James Connolly is given a Scottish accent and nothing other than unmistakably Irish voices are heard in the extensive scenes set in the GPO and on St Stephen's Green during Easter Week of 1916. Even Roddy Doyle's meticulously researched novel *A Star Called Henry*, published in 1999, fails to include any mention of the Kimmage garrison or the English and Scottish accents that filled the GPO on Easter Monday. While it expertly outlines the tensions between soldiers in the Citizen Army and those in the Irish Volunteers, Doyle was apparently unaware that those firing out of the GPO were anything but first generation Irish.

Today in the GPO, there are ten paintings hung around the main hall on the ground floor, the hall the rebels burst into nearly 90 years ago to start the Rising. The pictures depict various stages of the battle in the building, each accompanied by a short description of the events illustrated. Painting seven is of James Connolly, and includes a short biography. While it notes 'He spent several years in the US as a union organiser, before returning to Ireland in 1910,' it fails to mention his Scottish birth, or that he lived there for 20 years.

Second generation Irish figures like James Connolly, Tom Clarke, Mary MacSwiney, Maud Gonne, Countess Markievicz, Desmond Fitzgerald, Erskine Childers, Seán MacBride and Eamon de Valera were at the heart of the struggle for Irish independence in the first quarter of the last century. Some had to overcome prejudice about their birth or background from fellow republicans, and questions were asked about their loyalty.[25]

Doubts too were occasionally raised about Irish-born republicans whose bloodline was not obviously pure Celt. Cathal Brugha's father was from Yorkshire, and Padraig Pearse's from Nottingham. Pearse's mixed lineage and second generation Englishness caused him some serious angst.

> When my father and mother married there came together two very widely remote traditions. English and Puritan and mechanic on the one hand, Gaelic and Catholic and peasant on the other; freedom-loving both, and neither

> without its strain of poetry and its experience of spiritual and other adventure. And these two worked in me, and, fused together by a certain fire proper to myself, made me the strange thing that I am.[26]

Strange thing that he was, Pearse had an embarrassingly self-conscious open letter to himself printed in his newspaper *An Barr Buadh* in 1912. 'You don't make friends with the Gaels,' he wrote to himself. 'You avoid their company… Is it your English blood that is the cause of that, I wonder?'[27]

Whatever Pearse's sense of misfit, he was joined on Easter Monday 1916 in Dublin's General Post Office by dozens of second generation Irish Volunteers to help found the Republic.

3.
Cockney Rebels

It was a bright, cold Easter Monday morning. About eleven o'clock, 59 members of the Irish Volunteers boarded an open-top tram in the south Dublin suburb of Harold's Cross. 'Fifty-nine tupenny fares and don't stop 'til we reach O'Connell Bridge,' the officer in charge said to the driver, handing him the exact fare.[1]

Johnny O'Connor from south London played the flute and the men sang along on the top deck. O'Connor had such a strong Cockney accent that his nickname was 'Blimey' but the tunes he played were Irish and patriotic. The driver, perhaps intimidated by the top half of his tram being filled with men bulging with ammunition, ignored the cries of passengers who wanted to get off at their stops and sped straight to the city centre without pause. Most of the Volunteers on the tram, like O'Connor, had not been born or brought up in Ireland. Some had only been in the country a matter of weeks.[2]

They had joined Irish Volunteer companies in London, Glasgow, Liverpool and elsewhere and in the preceding months had quietly crossed over to Ireland to take part in the Rising. Séamus Reader of the Glasgow Volunteers had left Scotland on January 15 with six others, carrying one and a half hundredweight of explosives between them for the upcoming fight. Most of the Volunteers from across the sea slipped into

Dublin in ones and twos in the following months. Very few of them had relatives in the city, and so they set up the camp at Kimmage in south Dublin. There they busied themselves making hand grenades and ammunition and collecting other weapons to be used in the revolution.[3]

Laden with bandoleers, pick-axes, shovels, rifles and sledge-hammers, they clambered down the stairs of the tram when it finally stopped at O'Connell Bridge and made their way a few hundred yards along the river to Liberty Hall. There they were joined by about another hundred men, a mixture of Irish Volunteers and the Irish Citizen Army. 'Form fours!' ordered James Connolly, the general officer commanding Dublin, and the men, heavily laden with their weapons, struggled back towards the direction from where they had come, towards O'Connell Street. A couple of horse-drawn carts and a motor car helped carry the arsenal of rifles, pistols and shotguns. When they reached the General Post Office on the far side of the road, Connolly ordered them to 'Left turn!' and then 'Charge!' and the men crashed into the GPO, smashing windows and barricading the doors.[4]

Londoner Johnny 'Blimey' O'Connor was one of the first into the building.

> Oh! What excitement as we charged in. My throat was suddenly dry and immediately I got inside Tom Clarke handed me a tommy can. My first reaction was that the organisation must have been great to anticipate how thirsty we would get going into action… But I soon realised that the tommy can was in fact a home-made bomb.[5]

Thomas Clarke was the leader of the whole enterprise. His revolutionary career stretched back to the Fenian days of the previous century, when he had spent 15 years in British prisons for his part in a dynamite plot. Like O'Connor, he had been born in England, on the Isle of Wight. Clarke's early years had been spent in South Africa, where his father was a British soldier. He arrived in Ireland when he was about ten and, said his wife, 'was wildly excited, coming to a country which was interwoven into all his childhood dreams and imagination, a land of romance, heroism, a fairy land, where everything was beautiful'.[6]

Clarke's romanticism for Ireland had led to a lifetime of insurgency. By 1916 he was 59, the most senior republican in the Rising both in years and stature. He was head of the secret Irish Republican Brotherhood, the organisation that controlled the Volunteers and masterminded the Rising. His was the first name of seven leaders to appear at the bottom of the *Proclamation of the Republic* and he was, in his capacity as President of the Irish Republic, first into the GPO.[7]

It was about noon when Clarke led the men into the GPO, and within minutes customers had been cleared from the premises and the building was functioning as headquarters for the Volunteer leadership. Padraig Pearse, Joseph Plunkett, Connolly, Clarke and other key leaders of the republican movement stayed in the GPO. They were accompanied by between 100-150 men in the building, more than half of whom were from the Kimmage garrison. The 80 or 90 Volunteers who had been at Kimmage were known as 'The Refugees' because of their British origins, a nickname they resented. Elsewhere in the city, groups of other Volunteers seized strategic points in an effort to control and hold Dublin.

London-born Desmond Ryan had been Pearse's secretary, and was with him in the GPO. He described the garrison there as

> a formidable show. Some are glitteringly accoutred in trim grey-green, service rifle and automatic pistol, neatly rolled puttees, martial sabre, soldierly cap or dashing turned-up hat. Others – the majority – are merely in everyday garb, crossed and intercrossed with shoulder-straps, water-bottle, armed in many cases with shotguns or miniature rifles. Around their left arms, as a distinctive badge, they wear bright yellow bands.[8]

Shouts in Scouse, Mancunian, Glaswegian and Cockney accents echoed around the GPO as the men barricaded the windows. Blimey O'Connor took up a position at one of the windows next to the main door overlooking O'Connell Street as Pearse strode out to the pavement and read out the Proclamation of the Republic. A few hundred random passers-by milled about listening with varying degrees of interest and enthusiasm to Pearse, and some perfunctory cheers went up.[9]

Among those listening to Pearse was Margaret Skinnider, a maths teacher born and brought up in Glasgow, who had come over during her Easter holidays to take part in the Rising. Her parents were Irish, but had lived almost all of their lives in Scotland. In Glasgow Skinnider joined the Cumann na mBan, the women's section of the Volunteers, and had learned how to shoot a rifle. A few months before, during her Christmas break, she had visited Dublin for the first time and had made the ferry crossing with detonators stuffed under her coat, sleeping out on deck in the cold December wind scared that if she went below she 'might run into a hot-water pipe or an electric wire that would set them off'.[10]

Skinnider had spent most of the previous week scurrying around Dublin retrieving explosives and ammunition for use in the Rising, and had been assigned the duty of dispatch rider that Easter Monday. On her bicycle she shuttled the mile between the Volunteers at St Stephen's Green and the headquarters in O'Connell Street. As she arrived at the GPO with a message soon after noon she stopped and watched Pearse addressing the crowd.

Watching too from the street was Desmond Fitzgerald, who had rushed to the city centre when he heard the Rising had begun. Fitzgerald was born and grew up in east London, and as a teenager had changed his name from Tommy to Desmond because he fancied it sounded more romantic. 'In his mid-teens he was very influenced by Yeats. He joined the Gaelic League in London but his primary interest in Irish issues in those years was in poetry,' said his son Garret, who was Irish Taoiseach in the 1980s.[11]

Desmond Fitzgerald was married in St George's Cathedral in Southwark, and went to live in France. Then in 1913, 'for no tangible reason whatsoever, I felt either that there was going to be a great movement in Ireland, or that it was necessary that some movement should be launched,' he later recalled.[12]

Fitzgerald moved to the southwest corner of Ireland, near Dingle, where – to the bemusement of locals – the Cockney started a local company of Irish Volunteers with Ernest Blythe from Antrim. Despite their outsider status, the two did remarkably well in organising the Volunteers in West Kerry, much to the consternation of the local MP, Tom O'Donnell. On December 14 1915, O'Donnell spoke at a British military recruitment meeting in Dingle.

> In the course of his speech, O'Donnell mentioned strangers who had been visiting the district, and who were paid by German gold to lead the people astray. Having referred to Ernest Blythe and Desmond Fitzgerald, O'Donnell declared that if they ever came round again, he would ask them their real names; what their fathers' names were, and where they came from… His eloquence was of no avail, for there were no recruits to the Union Jack.[13]

Fitzgerald's activity led to a brief imprisonment, but he was free by the time of the Rising and had just arrived in O'Connell Street to hear Pearse announce the birth of the Republic. A few minutes later, Fitzgerald went into the GPO and was put in charge of food provisions, with strict instructions from Pearse to be as economical as possible with supplies.[14]

Fewer than 250 paces further down the street, one of O'Connor's mates from the London Volunteers, Joe Good, was sent to guard O'Connell Bridge. He was with two other Volunteers, Arthur Agnew from Liverpool and Paddy Moran from Glasgow. Good was 20 years old, and uncertain about his exact Irish ancestry. He was born in London and although his mother's name was Spencer, he believed she was Irish. He had spent 50 shillings to travel to Dublin two months before the Rising, his first visit to Ireland. Since then he had been part of the Kimmage outfit. 'Considering that most of our garrison had been born and bred in the heart of the empire, we were delightfully naïve in hoping to challenge the British Army,' he said.[15]

Armed only with an axe, Good stood with his back to the statue of Daniel O'Connell and, 'feeling somewhat foolish', looked across the River Liffey. He could hear the commotion at the GPO behind him. Some Volunteers had broken into Kelly's Gun shop on the corner of O'Connell Street and Bachelor's Walk, and called Good over to help them. He joined them in boring holes from one building to the next, as was the Volunteer plan, so they could step from house to house through adjoining walls without having to go onto the street.[16]

With picks and sledgehammers Good and his comrades smashed through the bricks and plaster of the shop to make a hole big enough for someone to crawl through into the next room, and then repeated the process to create a long 'tunnel' linking up with Volunteers further up O'Connell Street. Good had been smashing the walls for less than an hour when he was sent to the GPO with a rifle that had been found in Kelly's Gun Shop. He started out through the newly-bored tunnel but as it was still incomplete had to step out onto the pavement as he got nearer the GPO.[17]

Just as he did, a company of British Lancers on horseback charged down O'Connell Street towards the GPO. Blimey O'Connor and the men at the windows let fly with a barrage from an assortment of guns. Good threw himself on the ground. The Lancers scattered in disarray, four of them fatally wounded. O'Connor knew one of the injured British soldiers well, and had often met him socially in London.[18]

As Good returned to Kelly's after delivering his rifle, O'Connor was sent across the wide expanse of O'Connell Street to explore the possibility of rigging up a wireless transmitter. O'Connor and another qualified electrician from London, Liam Daley, rushed across the street and banged hard on the door of the wireless school, which had been occupied by Volunteers. 'When the Volunteer on duty heard our Cockney accents he refused to admit us,' said O'Connor, and for a while the two men from London were left standing on the pavement, dangerously exposed. Eventually they persuaded the guard they were on the same side, and O'Connor started searching for batteries and bits of equipment to make the receiver work. With Daley's help, he managed to build antennae on the roof of a building opposite the GPO to broadcast bulletins from James Connolly on the Rising's progress.[19]

Meanwhile, at the back of the GPO, the Nunan brothers from Brixton and two other Volunteers began to bore a hole through the wall to make a line of retreat. Teenagers Sean and Ernie Nunan had been sent to Ireland by their father, an IRB man, to take part in the Rising. The Volunteers eventually broke into the waxworks in Henry St, where they found dummies of King George V and Lord Kitchener. Declaring them 'prisoners of war' they carried them back to the GPO and used them to shore up the barricades. Nothing better symbolised the apparent incongruity of the London Volunteers in O'Connell Street than the waxworks cameo: two young south London boys, fighting for an Irish Republic, carrying back to their headquarters an effigy of Lord Kitchener, the British Minister for War, who was born and raised in County Kerry.[20]

That evening, looting by civilians of the shops in and around O'Connell Street began in earnest. Sean Nunan watched, bemused from the GPO, and saw one of the looters 'going along with a dress suit on him and he had a golf club'. Meanwhile, Joe Good looked down from his position on the roof of Kelly's Gun Shop. 'At one time I had clear sight of some of our Kimmage lads among the small group of Volunteers trying to restrain the looters,' he recalled. 'It was amusing to imagine the tone and accents of some of our Cockney or Liverpudlian admonitions to those celebratory citizens of this newly taken "Fair City". To these Dubliners they would have sounded more alien than the voices of Irishmen in the British army.'[21]

That night, few Volunteers in O'Connell Street or elsewhere in the city slept. O'Connor and a few others worked all night to get the radio working in the wireless school and just before dawn managed to send out an optimistic message announcing 'An Irish Republic has been proclaimed. Dublin has been held and all

British attacks have been repulsed'. Across the road in the GPO the electricity had been cut, so the men sang in the dark as the rain lashed down outside. The favourite song was *The Soldier's Song*. Written in 1907, it was eventually to become the Republic of Ireland's national anthem. For many in the building the second line held particular significance.

> Soldiers are we, whose lives are pledged to Ireland,
> Some have come from a land beyond the wave,
> Sworn to be free, no more an ancient sireland
> Shall shelter the despot or the slave.[22]

The next morning looting resumed on a larger scale, with Volunteers at a loss to prevent it. Joe Good found a sword at Kelly's, and decided to take it to his friend Mick Collins when he next went to the GPO with messages. It was exactly two years to the day since he and Collins had been sworn into the London Volunteers together. Good knew Collins from the London Irish scene, and had first encountered the Corkman when he saw him cheating in a running race organised by the Gaelic Athletic Association at Herne Hill in southeast London.[23]

Collins, a few years older than Good, had moved to London from Clonakilty in 1906, when he was 15. He had spent almost all of his adult life in the British capital and had been drilled with Good, Blimey O'Connor and the London Volunteers every week either at the German gymnasium in King's Cross or later, when the north and south London units of the Volunteers merged, in the parish hall of St George's Cathedral in Southwark. Provision had been made for British-based Volunteers when the organisation's constitution was passed in October 1914. 'Every body of Irishmen, whether in Ireland or abroad who band themselves together to attain the stated objects, who sign the enrolment form, and who subscribe to the constitution of the Irish Volunteers will be eligible for recognition as a corps of Irish Volunteers…' Within a year the Irish Volunteer newspaper reported that among the first areas which had elected representatives to the Volunteer council were those in Scotland

and the North of England.[24]

The London Volunteers' drill instructor was Louis Noble, who had served as a sergeant in the British Army. Noble was born in Hertfordshire, outside London, and had lived all his life in England, but his mother was Irish and he played the bagpipes. He was well known at London-Irish music festivals, and his military experience made him an obvious choice to drill the Volunteers.[25]

Collins had left London in mid-January and became part of the Kimmage unit, and although he did not sleep at the camp, he was there virtually every day. The Volunteers from Britain didn't know what to make of Collins. Some resented his overbearing attitude, but others were grateful for the second-hand clothes he foraged for them when they were camped at Kimmage. On the tram trip into town that morning he had sat imperiously in his full Volunteer outfit, ignoring the sniggers of his comrades, most of whose only 'uniform' was a military badge or cap worn with civvies.[26]

Good found Collins on the ground floor of the GPO and gave him the sword as a peace offering – Good had teased Collins more than most at Kimmage. He took the opportunity to have a quick look around the headquarters and was surprised at how many women had reinforced the garrison there. He hurried back to his post at Kelly's and spent another stressful night there, waiting for the British to attack.[27]

He didn't have to wait long. The next morning artillery shelling of suspected Volunteer strongholds began. Shells blasted into Kelly's shop where Good and his comrades dived for cover, shaken by the ferocity of the assault. Tired and hungry (he had only dozed in snatches and eaten pieces of chocolate since Monday morning), Good was ordered to the GPO to report the situation. Disguised as a priest, he had to ask directions from locals on the roundabout route he was forced to take to avoid the gunfire. He was ordered to go back to Kelly's and tell the men there to retreat to the GPO, which he did.

The shelling also interfered with O'Connor and the detail assigned to the wireless school. O'Connor tried to persuade Connolly to let him bring the radio gear over from the school to the GPO, and initially Connolly agreed, but when he saw the amount of equipment needed would necessitate six or more trips across O'Connell Street, he cancelled the plan.[28]

Meanwhile, reinforcements were sent from the GPO to the nearby Imperial Hotel, where W.J. Brennan-Whitmore was in command. 'The group had in it Capt. Frank Thornton who arrived in full Volunteer uniform,' he recalled, and knew Thornton was part of the Kimmage garrison over from England. 'They were somewhat humorously referred to as "the refugees",' he said. 'No braver or better body of Irishmen existed.'[29]

Over at St Stephen's Green, Volunteers and members of the Irish Citizen Army under Michael Mallin and Countess Markievicz had been engaged in serious combat with the British. Margaret Skinnider had spent the previous few days as part of the Volunteer force there, listening to the Countess issuing orders in her posh English accent. Born into an upper-class family at a fashionable London address 48 years earlier, Constance Markievicz made an unlikely hero of the Irish proletariat. She had Irish relatives in Sligo, but had been very much part of the elite London scene. The daughters of Sir Henry Gore-Booth, she and her sister Eva had been presented at court in the usual way for women of her station, and had for years spent 'the season' in London. Constance had married a Polish count at a London society wedding, and had later converted to socialism and Irish republicanism.[30]

Markievicz had joined Connolly's Citizen Army, and – in keeping with his views on women's equality – had been made a commandant. For the early part of Easter week the woman who had once curtsied before Queen Victoria directed troops around St Stephen's Green dressed in full uniform, a gun slung from either hip, and a spray of feathers bursting from her black velour hat.[31]

By Wednesday afternoon, Markievicz, Mallin and the rebel contingent had moved into the College of Surgeons, overlooking the green. Markievicz gave Skinnider a Citizen Army uniform. Skinnider recalled:

> It consisted of kneebreeches, belted coat, and puttees. I slipped into this uniform, climbed up astride the rafters, and was assigned a loophole through which to shoot. It was dark there, full of smoke and the din of firing, but it was good to be in action. I could look across the tops of the trees and see the British soldiers on the roof of the Shelbourne [Hotel]. I could also hear their shots hailing against the roof and wall of our fortress, for in truth this building was just that. More than once I saw the man I aimed at fall.[32]

That evening, Skinnider was upstairs in the College of Surgeons,

> studying a map of our surroundings and trying to find a way by which we could dislodge the soldiers from the roof of the Shelbourne. When Commandant Mallin came in, I asked him if he would let me go out with one man and try to throw a bomb attached to an eight-second fuse through the hotel window… We could use our bicycles and get away before the bomb exploded – that is, if we were quick enough… Commandant Mallin agreed the plan was a good one, but much too dangerous. I pointed out to him that it had been my speed which had saved me so far from machine-gun fire on the hotel roof.[33]

After further lobbying from Skinnider, Mallin reluctantly agreed to the scheme, on condition that she first cut off the line of retreat for a group of British soldiers who had installed a gun on the top of a church. Skinnider and four men went to set fire to a building to prevent the soldiers escaping.

> It took only a few moments to reach the building we were to set afire. [Volunteer] William Partridge used the butt of his rifle to smash the glass door in the front of a shop that occupied the ground floor. As he did, the rifle went off. 'I rushed past him into the doorway of the shop, calling to the others to come on. Behind me came the sound of a volley and I fell… The flash had revealed us to the enemy. 'It's all over,' I muttered, as I felt myself falling.[34]

Volunteer Fred Ryan fell dead next to her. Partridge carried her back to the college. 'They laid me on a large table and cut away the coat of my fine, new uniform. I cried over that. Then they found I had been shot in three places…' she recalled. Markievicz held her hand as another woman dug bullets out of her right arm, right side and back. Skinnider didn't utter a sound during the operation. Markievicz sneaked out and returned a few minutes later. 'Don't worry, Margaret my dear,' she said. 'I got the wretched blighter for you.'[35]

The next morning, the mood in the GPO was bright. Some spoke of holding out for several more days and perhaps weeks. Cockney electrician Liam Daley sent Good to the roof of the GPO to repair the telephone lines laid a few days earlier by Blimey O'Connor. 'I made the repair hurriedly and lay very flat, hoping that my posterior would not be observed above the low balustrade,' he said. Good got down from the roof before the first shells hit the building. Pearse tried to raise morale by assembling the men for a pep talk. Good, unimpressed, thought Pearse had 'shot his bolt'.[36]

On Friday morning, it was Connolly's turn to rally the troops. He had been wounded earlier in the week, and was propped up in a bed to address them. His speech to the Volunteers went down much better, but incendiary shells soon began to rain onto the roof of the building, threatening to turn the GPO into a fireball. By the afternoon most of O'Connell Street was ablaze, and Volunteers stationed in surrounding buildings fled back to the GPO. About a dozen from the Metropol Hotel made their way into headquarters. Inside the GPO, a shotgun went off accidentally – not for the first time that week – and hit Volunteer Andrew Furlong's ammunition pouch. Bullets flew everywhere – including nine into Furlong's leg – and London Volunteer Neale was hit. A Cockney and a socialist, Neale was famous for calling everyone 'comrade'. He swayed and was put down on pile of mail bags. 'I'm dying, comrade,' he said simply.[37]

The leaders decided to evacuate. At 6pm sixteen of the wounded men and twelve of the fifteen women still left in the

GPO abandoned it for the nearby Coliseum Theatre in Henry Street. Fitzgerald went with them, as did Peggy Downey, a Liverpudlian who had helped him in the headquarters kitchen. As the injured men tried to get comfortable in the theatre bar Fitzgerald ordered them not to touch any of the alcohol. Fitzgerald's ban did little to improve his popularity rating.[38]

Many had complained about his miserly food rations during the week, and clashes over his portions were not uncommon. One encounter had been with a party of London Volunteers. 'Mick Collins… strode in one evening with some of his men who were covered with dust and had been demolishing walls or building barricades,' he remembered. '[He] announced these men were to be fed if they took the last food in the place. I did not attempt to argue with him, and the men sat down, openly rejoicing that I had been crushed.'[39]

Pearse, Connolly, Clarke and the last few rebels left the GPO and made for a nearby house. Good was with them. 'Connolly was being taken into this small house and was being carried upstairs on a stretcher,' recalled Good. 'I gave a hand on the narrow staircase, so narrow that Connolly was sometimes perpendicular… He remained calm, though he was obviously in extreme pain, and remarked, "A heavy load, chum," recognising my London accent.' Connolly himself spoke in a Scottish accent, having been born and brought up in Edinburgh.[40]

The son of Irish parents, James Connolly was 48 at the time of the Rising. He had spent most of his life living in Scotland and the US, and his first experience of Ireland had been as a soldier in the British Army's occupying force. Connolly spent seven years as a British soldier in Ireland as part of the King's Liverpool Regiment. He later moved to Ireland at the age of 27 to promote socialism, and in time had come to lead the socialist movement and the Irish Citizen Army founded by his mentor, James Larkin of Liverpool. The legendary labour leader Jim Larkin, like Connolly, was second generation Irish, and had moved to Dublin from Liverpool at the age of 31. He was in the

US at the time of the Rising.[41]

Good stayed with Connolly and the other exhausted leaders throughout Friday night. The next morning surrender seemed inevitable. Connolly, Pearse and Plunkett huddled together and discussed their limited options. They asked Good to go and find Tom Clarke. 'I went and found Tom,' he recalled. 'He was standing near a window, silent and alone. A quiet, gentle little man, there was nothing in his appearance to suggest that he was an old Fenian of the earlier generation. And yet, he was the Revolution.'[42] One stage of the revolution was about to end. Good watched the pretty, pale Elizabeth O'Farrell carefully walk up the street carrying the republicans' white flag of surrender.

As negotiations over the surrender procedure developed, it became clear that the British, and in particular General Lowe, were primarily interested in the whereabouts of the British-born Constance Markievicz and James Connolly. Markievicz was still fighting in St. Stephen's Green, while Connolly was sitting up in bed shaving himself in preparation for handing himself over to the enemy. As he shaved, his secretary asked him what would happen to the Kimmage lads. Good could not make out his reply, but it was an ominous question.[43] The Kimmage garrison, because they were either British-born or had been living in Britain the previous year, believed they were in greater danger than their comrades because they had evaded conscription to the British Army. The *Military Service Act* of 1915 stipulated that all men of military service age in Britain were liable for conscription. The law did not apply to Ireland, so while those Volunteers who were from Ireland could not be prosecuted or press-ganged into the British Army under the Act, the Volunteers from London, Glasgow and Liverpool could.

Talk of surrender made Good and the rest of the Kimmage garrison furious. Believing they had nothing to lose, they wanted to carry on the fight. A split emerged between hard-core, British-born Volunteers who refused to surrender, and the Irish-born Volunteers.

> The situation was serious, and bordered on something close to mutiny. [The British-born] believed that if they surrendered they would all be treated as deserters, most of them having English accents. They said that if they were in danger of being shot as deserters they would prefer to be killed still fighting the British army. Many others believed they would be conscripted if captured, and anything was preferable to that. I was sympathetic; I had an English accent myself and believed with them that our position was the least enviable of any who surrendered.[44]

Some of the men from London refused to surrender. First Tom Clarke tried to persuade them to give up. He spoke to them at great length, assuring them that only himself and the leaders would be shot, not the British-born contingent. Despite his impressive speech and impeccable reputation, he failed to persuade them. Mick Collins, who knew the Londoners very well, was despatched to try next. He was at his belligerent best, urging them to see sense, but even Collins could not sway them. Then Joe Plunkett had a go. At the point of death himself from illness, he pleaded with them to lay down their arms. They would not be moved.

Then it was the turn of Sean MacDiarmada, one of those whose name appeared at the bottom of the Proclamation of the Republic. Instead of talking to the men, he listened.

> He listened very, very carefully, with a sort of charmed concentration. And then he began to speak, very quietly, with enormous concentration… He told us that the worst that would happen to the Irish Volunteers from England would be 'a few years' in jail…The thing you must do, all of you, is to survive …We, who will be shot, will die happy – knowing that there are still plenty of you around who will finish the job.[45]

It worked. The Rising was over.

Joe Plunkett walked out onto Moore Street waving a white flag, but not all the British appeared to realise what was happening, and some snipers carried on shooting, making it difficult for the Volunteers to evacuate the wounded. Plunkett sent Good to the nearby British barricade to explain the problem. Good found a British officer. 'He waited for me to speak, but I remained silent until he addressed me himself. Taking some care to diminish my London accent, I then delivered my message…'[46]

Word was spreading to Volunteer outposts in the city and throughout the country of the surrender. Piaras Béaslaí had been born and educated in Liverpool, and had moved to Dublin at the age of 23. Prominent since the very earliest days of the Volunteers, he had been Vice-Commandant of the 1st Dublin Battalion of the Volunteers in North King Street, and surrendered with his men at 10pm that night. In Galway, word eventually reached 23 year-old Liam Mellows that the fight was over. He had led several hundred men in several skirmishes across the county. Mellows had joined the IRB in 1911 when he walked into Tom Clarke's tobacconist shop in north Dublin. He told Clarke his background – that he had been born in England because his father was in the British Army but was eager to fight for Ireland. Clarke was touched by his story because it so closely mirrored his own, and had taken a special interest in Mellows.[47]

Slowly, the rebels began to turn themselves in. A few lucky ones, like Mellows, got away. Margaret Skinnider, who been hit by three bullets at St. Stephen's Green, also escaped. She had been patched up and sent to St. Vincent's Hospital, where she was arrested by the British. A doctor interceded, contacting Dublin Castle and telling the authorities she was in no state to be imprisoned. She was released, and slipped away to Scotland.[48]

The British found that many of their prisoners didn't have Irish accents. Although those who fought for Ireland that Easter week were not exactly an international brigade, there were – excluding those born in Britain – some foreigners among them. Fitzgerald recalled that soon after entering the GPO, 'While I was on the ground floor, two smiling Swedes came up. They explained that they had heard we were fighting the English, and as they did not like the English they had come to join. But they belonged to a ship that was sailing on Thursday, and they would have to leave in time to catch it.' There are similar reports of foreign sailors from Poland and Finland being allowed into the GPO to help. On Easter Monday, the first day of the Rising, a dozen or so Americans from the Hibernian Rifles joined the men in the GPO, and their number grew to about 30 as the Rising went on.[49]

The most famous American-born rebel was Eamon de Valera. He had been born in New York City to a Spanish father and Irish mother 33 years before the Easter Rising. His father had left his mother shortly after the boy's birth, and died a couple of years later. His mother, apparently believing her son's best chances lay back in Ireland, sent him to be brought up by her family in the village of Bruree in Limerick at the age of three.[50]

He had won a series of scholarships and by 1916 had enjoyed more formal education than most Volunteers. He commanded the Volunteer garrison at Boland's Mill in the south of Dublin city during Easter week, and – as a senior officer – was duly sentenced to death. De Valera's mother in New York and his wife in Dublin tried to plead of his behalf with the American authorities, claiming that his New York birth afforded him the protection of American citizenship. A campaign was quickly put together, with various American politicians trying to intercede on his behalf. Whatever the effectiveness of his family's efforts, de Valera's death sentence was lifted, and he was sentenced to penal servitude for life instead. The idea that de Valera's life was spared because of his American birth is still popular in Ireland, although there is persuasive evidence that the British authorities, in response to internal and international protests against the executions, decided to execute James Connolly and then stop.[51]

The other leaders were not so fortunate. Those whose names appeared under the *Proclamation of the Republic*, and other perceived ringleaders, were shot by firing squad. In the obituaries of James Connolly, reports of his origins were confused. The *Irish Times* first reported that he had been born in

Cork, then later amended that to Monaghan. The *Cork Examiner* mentioned Scotland, then changed that to 'the north of England'. Both local Isle of Wight papers covered the Rising, but neither mentioned that its leader, Thomas Clarke, had been born there.[52]

The other captured Volunteers were sent to prisons in England and Wales. For those prisoners not born in Ireland there was the real fear that they would be brought before courts martial and tried as deserters from the *Conscription Act*. Vigorous efforts were made by the prison authorities to find out which prisoners were liable for conscription, which generated some animosity towards the 'refugees' from some Irish-born prisoners. Fellow republican prisoner Joe O'Reilly explained:

> Some of the other prisoners (who had not fought [in the Rising]) blamed the refugees for causing all the trouble. Certain refugees met to consider whether they should give themselves up. Mick [Collins] burst in on the meeting and sat down. When he heard their proposition he told them to do nothing of the kind but sit tight, and not to mind the cowards.

The Volunteers stuck together and refused to identify themselves in a 'No Names, No Numbers' campaign.'[53]

Eventually, the Nunan brothers from London, the King brothers (George and Paddy) from Liverpool and Paddy O'Donoghue were discovered and sent for trial. Ernest and Sean Nunan were sent from their prison at Frongoch in Wales to London's Wormwood Scrubs for the hearing under the *Military Service Act*. Sean was found guilty and ordered to join the British Army. He refused, and was sent to prison. Ernie was actually found to be too young to be conscripted into the British Army, but a few months later, when he had reached 18, was retried. He was ordered to put on a British uniform, refused and so was also imprisoned. He was finally released in February 1917 with a 'bad conduct' discharge. The others who were tried and refused to join the British Army all went to prison and were eventually discharged for 'not being likely to give loyal and faithful service to His Majesty'. Others, like Joe Good, avoided detection and were never drafted into the British military, but he remained 'ever-conscious of the threat that hung over me that I would be picked out and have to go through the ordeal of defying the British Army alone'.[54]

Nearly all of the republican prisoners were released from the jails in England and Wales by Christmas. Most of the British-born Volunteers returned to Ireland, and many immediately signed up for IRA service.

4.
Fighting the Empire

As skirmishes between the IRA and the police and British Army turned into full-blown guerrilla war in the following years, British-born Volunteers continued to play key roles in the fight for independence. Although he had only ever spent three months in Ireland, Joe Good regarded it as his home, and joined the Second Battalion of C Company of the Dublin Volunteers immediately after his release from prison in Wales. Louis Noble, the piper who had been recruited by Collins in early 1914 to drill Nunan and the other London Volunteers, had stayed in London during the Rising, and used his position as an electrician in Acton to supply special wire for munitions to the Dublin IRA. Eventually, he decided to leave England and get closer to the action.

> I put all my home into a repository at Hammersmith and then went to Belfast. I stopped there with James McCann, and Art Agnew who was a 1916 man from Liverpool who introduced me to Sean O'Neill, who after writing to Michael Collins about me admitted me into the IRA. I was made Adjutant of the Engineers Co. With Andy Furlong as OC I carried out training and instruction work with infantry and engineers on Divis Mountain and at Straid, Co. Antrim.

Noble later moved to Dublin, joined the 5th Battalion, and was posted to No. 2 Company. His London accent proved a dangerous asset on several occasions, he said, including once where an IRA man, believing him to be a British detective, pulled a gun on him and nearly shot him.[1]

For other Volunteers, an English accent proved a distinct advantage. Liverpudlian John Pinkman was 16 when he joined the Roger Casement Sinn Féin club in the city in 1918. His cousin, Bernie Meehan from Sligo, had been arrested for his part in the Rising two years before and Pinkman was keen to see military action. He helped raid a gun shop in Liverpool for the IRA, but when it was suggested he should go and join the fight in Dublin, the teenage Pinkman hesitated. 'To tell the truth, I was afraid of my mother and what she'd say to me if I told her I was going off to Dublin,' he admitted.[2]

Pinkman stayed in Liverpool, drilling with the Volunteers at night on the Grand National racecourse at Aintree, and planning sabotage. At the end of 1920, he helped burn down a large part of Liverpool docks. 'I remained on the lookout, because if it were necessary to speak to a passer-by, my Liverpool accent would not arouse the suspicion that an Irish brogue would,' he said. Huge damage was done in the fire – news reports estimated that all the timber yards and warehouses along an eight-mile stretch of the docks had been destroyed. Millions of pounds of damage had been done, and an 18 year-old dock labourer killed.[3]

Pinkman was eventually arrested and sentenced to five years' penal servitude for his part in burning farmhouses near Liverpool as reprisals for the damage being done in Ireland by British Black and Tan soldiers. During his trial his English birth became something of an issue when the police report of his interrogation was read out.

> Detective-Sergeant Moffat, the chief witness for the prosecution… said that at the time of my arrest he noticed I spoke with an English accent and asked me if I was an Englishman.
>
> 'No', I said. 'I'm Irish and proud of it, too.'
> 'An Irishman born in England?' he asked sarcastically.

'Yes', I said, 'unfortunately!'

The exchange made the papers the following day.[4]

Pinkman's activities in Liverpool were part of a wider republican assault on Britain. Although most Volunteer units in Britain collapsed after 1916 because their members went to participate in the Easter Rising, they began to reorganise in 1919 and 1920 in Liverpool, Tyneside, Manchester, London, Sheffield, Birmingham, Glasgow and Edinburgh. As Peter Hart has chronicled, they were responsible for several high-profile incidents, including the escape from Lincoln Jail in February 1919 of de Valera, and another breakout of republican prisoners from prison in Manchester seven months later. Mass arson attacks on often random property targets were carried out in London suburbs, Manchester and the Liverpool docks.[5]

IRA units in Britain gathered the home addresses of British military personnel serving in Ireland, and at least fifteen addresses were attacked and five people, relatives of British Auxiliaries, were shot and many houses burned. 'On average,' Hart has calculated in a study of the IRA in Britain during this period, 'IRA incidents were taking place twice a day in Britain, concentrated in and around London, Manchester and Newcastle' between January and July 1921, and between the summers of 1920 and 1921 there were about 1000 men enrolled in British IRA units.[6]

Hart suggests that this IRA organisation 'was as much a British as an Irish movement, largely composed of people who had been born or brought up in England and Scotland, or who had settled there as employed and permanent residents.'[7]

Desmond Fitzgerald's London-born brother France provided explosives to Michael Collins from his chemical works in east London. Desmond Fitzgerald and Liverpudlian Piaras Béaslaí were elected to the Dáil in the elections of 1918. Béaslaí became TD for East Kerry, Fitzgerald for the Dublin constituency of Pembroke. Both were arrested during the War for Independence. Béaslaí escaped from Mountjoy in broad daylight using a rope ladder in the spring of 1919, and then – when rearrested and jailed in Strangeways – escaped from the Manchester prison in October of that year. Fitzgerald and Béaslaí were key figures in republican publicity and propaganda during this period, and rose to the top echelons of the movement. Béaslaí edited the IRA newspaper *An t-Óglach* (The Soldier), and Fitzgerald was made Minister of Propaganda.

Béaslaí's celebrated Mountjoy escape in March 1919 was helped by Sean Nunan of Brixton, and a month later Nunan joined Michael Collins in one of the war's most daring escapades – both were smuggled into police headquarters at Brunswick Street by Collins' inside agent Ned Broy. Collins and Nunan spent the whole night locked inside a small room on the top floor of the offices, rifling through the police intelligence files on Sinn Féin. In the small hours Nunan looked up when he heard Collins chuckling over a report on Collins himself, dated December 31, 1916 and submitted by a detective in Bandon, which started with the line, 'He comes from a brainy Cork family'.[8]

Joe Good, meanwhile, was assigned a more direct military role. In early 1918 a conscription crisis gripped Ireland. Many feared that Britain would extend its policy of military conscription to young men in Ireland, a move which some warned would result in widespread bloodshed. Republicans promised to resist any efforts to conscript men in Ireland, although some believed Britain was bluffing and would never try to compel Irishmen in Ireland to join its army.

> It was suggested then that the British government intended imposing conscription in Ireland to crush Sinn Féin. This was my own view, since I had been born and brought up in London. Irish-born people did not understand that Englishmen regarded Irishmen as fellow-Britishers, somewhat rowdy, but good fellows when disciplined…[9]

By April 1918 Good was working, somewhat ironically, at a munitions factory in Dublin, making weapons for the British war effort. Several Volunteers worked in the factory, doing their best to be as inefficient as possible. He was summoned to IRA headquarters and asked by Cathal Brugha if he was prepared to take on a dangerous mission. He had already guessed what it was – to assassinate members of the British cabinet to deter the government from introducing conscription to Ireland. Brugha was to head the team of ten assassins in London. Good was given five pounds and told to take the boat and train to the British capital. The safe houses Good and the others were supposed to stay in did not work out, and Good had to find places among his London contacts for the republicans. He stayed at the Nunans' house in the south of the city.[10]

Each of the men was assigned a member of the war cabinet to tail and eventually kill. Good was given the leader of the Conservative Party, Andrew Bonar Law. 'I had nothing against Bonar Law except that he was fond of matinees,' said Good. 'We were to be often at the theatre together and I got to know his habits well, though he, of course, was unaware of the existence of his escort.' The rest of the time, the assassins trudged the streets of London in pairs. Brugha once got them all together for a meeting in Regent's Park, but Good was shocked at his leader's Dublin ways, which he thought horribly conspicuous. 'I gasped when he came riding his bicycle along the paths, as though he were in Dublin's Phoenix Park,' he said, and was horrified that Brugha walked around London wearing bicycle clips and carrying a pump, and had a 'mode of behaviour and appearance peculiar to Dublin but very rare in London'.[11]

Though Brugha's lack of London street wisdom worried Good, he never doubted the man's commitment. 'Around that time I'd begun to be aware of a fascinating connection, a common factor shared by men like Cathal [Brugha], P.H. Pearse and even de Valera. They all had Irish mothers. Perhaps, because they were half-Irish, a tension bred from their mixed origins made them all zealots …'[12]

Eventually, after a series of false alerts – including one when most of the team went to the House of Commons fully armed – the mission was abandoned. Britain never attempted to impose conscription in Ireland.

Good returned to Ireland and busied himself helping an IRA flying column in Limerick and picking up intelligence through casual conversations with British soldiers – '... my London accent made it easy for me to communicate with British soldiers. There has always been a naïve assumption that an English accent precludes any Irish republican allegiance,' he said. Capitalising on this assumption, Good boldly walked into Beggar's Bush barracks in the south of Dublin and offered his services as an electrician. The plan came to nothing, but Good spent a valuable day picking up information from inside one of the key British military installations in the city. 'No one in that barracks that day had thought me to be anything other than British,' he recalled.[13]

After years of ambush, assassination and atrocities, a truce was finally declared in July 1921, and negotiations between the republicans and the British government began. Although de Valera was President of Sinn Féin, he had decided not to take direct part in the negotiations.

Instead, a team was despatched to negotiate with the British government. They were Arthur Griffith, Michael Collins, G. Gavan Duffy, E.J. Duggan and Robert Barton. Fitzgerald accompanied them as a relatively junior member, and was not officially a delegate (or plenipotentiary, as they were known). Nevertheless, according to one commentator, Fitzgerald appears to have added a dash of glamour to the outfit, as 'he enjoyed a unique position among British and foreign journalists, with his youth, his looks, his combination of literary grace and wit with ferocious activity and endurance, of gaiety with fixed resolve'.[14]

It was Barton's English-born cousin Erskine Childers, who was an official secretary to the Irish delegation, who cut a far more controversial figure. Born in London to an upper-class family, Childers' mother was from Wicklow. He appeared quintessentially English, and by 1921 had enjoyed a curious path to Irish republicanism. True, he had helped arm the Volunteers by gun-running a small yacht full of weapons to Howth in 1914, but before that he had elected to join the British Army to defend the Empire against the Boer uprising in South Africa. When the Great War broke out, he immediately signed up for service in the British military and – thanks to his novel *The Riddle of the Sands* – was acknowledged as an expert with few peers on the British navy.

Yet despite his upper-class English upbringing and education (he had gone to the exclusive public school Haileybury and Trinity College, Cambridge), he had retained – through Barton and his Wicklow cousins – some affection for Ireland. His wife explained that some time in early 1919 '…we gradually decided to give ourselves to Ireland. You may notice that we both think of ourselves British or English. Erskine may still use the word "us" in that way.'[15]

As 1919 unfolded, Childers rose meteorically in Sinn Féin. His cousin Barton – who was on the run – introduced him to Collins and, impressed with his education and credentials, Collins, Griffith and Fitzgerald asked him to press Ireland's case at the postwar Paris Peace Conference. By the end of the year Childers had moved to Dublin and, with Fitzgerald, reorganised Sinn Féin's publicity department. When Fitzgerald was arrested, de Valera made Childers Minister for Propaganda, even though he wasn't a member of the Dáil, and de Valera even said Childers was 'the model of all I'd wish to have been myself.'[16]

Not everyone was so impressed. Griffith regarded Childers as 'a disgruntled Englishman'. Beaslaí assessed that Childers 'carried weight as an outsider, with an English-made reputation, which he could not have carried on his own merits, had he been an Irishman in the movement for years and finding his own level'.[17]

By the end of 1921 Childers was a hardline republican who had been elected to the Dáil and had had a spell on the run. In December he found himself sitting between Arthur Griffith and E.J. Duggan in the cabinet room at 10 Downing Street as part of the Irish delegation. On the opposite side of the table were the British representatives, including Childers' old school chum Lionel Curtis, Winston Churchill and Churchill's secretary Eddie Marsh, who Childers had taught to flyfish while they were at Cambridge together. Childers' rigid focus and dedication to the cause meant he avoided Curtis' eye and pretended not to recognise Marsh. Further along the table sat British Prime Minister Lloyd George, whom Childers also knew from his days as clerk of the House of Commons. In fact, it hadn't been that many years before that Childers and Lloyd George used to stroll to work together along the south bank of the Thames.[18]

Although Childers was only the delegation's official secretary and could not vote, the British tried to have him excluded from some of the session because he was regarded as the most uncompromising and extreme of the republicans, and his hardline dedication to republicanism caused strains in the Irish team, not least with Griffith.

A deal was eventually, and controversially, struck between the negotiating teams, and became known as the Treaty. Childers, predictably, was against it as it involved compromise. It was Fitzgerald who arrived from London carrying the Treaty and presented it to de Valera in Dublin. Fitzgerald was horrified to discover that de Valera intended to reject the agreement.

De Valera and much of the Irish public and IRA were bitterly disappointed that the deal fell short of their expectation of a full republic. The debates in the Dáil over the Treaty exposed the bitterness that would eventually ignite the Civil War. Attacked for having signed something less than a full republic, Collins lashed out at his critics in a series of abusive exchanges on the floor of the Dáil.

Searching for wounding rhetoric to counter those who accused him of betraying the republic, Collins angrily attacked the anti-Treaty TDs sitting opposite him. 'Deserters all to the Irish nation in her hour of trial. We will stand by her,' he sputtered. Spying de Valera, Markievicz and others, he searched for the ultimate insult 'Foreigners – Americans – English!' he shouted. Griffith took up the cudgel. Responding to criticisms from Childers, he snapped 'I will not reply to any damned Englishman in this assembly.'[19]

5.

Fighting Ourselves

Bitter political debate became Civil War. Irish- and foreign-born IRA Volunteers split to both sides of the divide. Fitzgerald and Béaslaí supported Collins and the Treaty. Others, like Childers and Markievicz, rejected it and coalesced around de Valera.

Following skirmishes between the two factions throughout the country, the anti-Treaty forces took over the Four Courts building in central Dublin and tried to hold out against Collins' new Free State Army. The zealous Childers, ready to fight for the republic, found it difficult to join an IRA unit as no commander wanted him. Too often regarded as foreign and different, his upper class manners compounded his misfit image. He once interrupted a meeting of rural flying column leaders to politely inquire where the toilet was.[1]

Fitzgerald and Béaslaí, so effective as propagandists in the war with England, now turned their talents on the anti-Treaty IRA, or Irregulars, as Béaslaí dubbed them. He became a Major General in the Free State Army, and toured the US in 1922 to generate support for the Treaty.

Cockneys Blimey O'Connor and Louis Noble, who had both known Collins well in London, opposed him and the Treaty.

Noble had no hesitation in taking up arms against the new Irish Free State.

> When the split in my company due to the treaty came I took charge of the company at Lourdes Home, Buckingham Street. When the Four Courts was attacked I reported to Liam O'Doherty at Moran's Hotel. I was put in charge of the basement kitchen and wine cellar, and took charge of a party to cut holes in the walls in the rear for the retreat. I then went with a party to the Gresham Hotel [in O'Connell Street, opposite the GPO] to Cathal Brugha; there I was engaged in making mines and on ambulance work, and on the fall of these positions I was wounded going to the assistance of Cathal Brugha… the same volley that I got killed him.[2]

Liverpudlian John Pinkman was among the Free State soldiers who attacked Noble and Brugha. Pinkman and some of his Liverpool IRA colleagues had made straight for Dublin on their release from prison in Dartmoor. They had not been there long when they heard talk of a new Free State Army being formed. 'We'd already seen a few of the soldiers in their green uniforms and when someone suggested we should all join up together it sounded like a great idea. We agreed that since Ireland was building a real army of its own we who had been Volunteers should be among the first to join it,' he recalled.[3]

Pinkman walked into Beggar's Bush barracks on March 1, 1922 and signed up. Despite misgivings about the lack of discipline and professionalism in the new army, and its apparent aping of too many British military traditions, Pinkman became an enthusiastic regular soldier. In July he was part of a detail sent to flush out IRA men in Moran's Hotel – the group that included Noble and Brugha. Pinkman also saw an old republican friend from Liverpool in the vicinity. 'I recognised him as Donal Mulhall, a former member of the Liverpool Company, and shook my head sadly. He was wearing a civilian suit of tweeds with a Red Cross band tied around his right arm – no knapsack of first-aid supplies, or anything like that. I felt certain he was one of the [IRA] gang that had escaped through the back door of Moran's.'[4]

After the gun battle that soon followed, the wounded Noble was taken prisoner and marched to Amiens Street Station, from where he escaped. He went to St. Vincent's Hospital for an operation on his bullet wounds, and was incapacitated for two months. He based himself in the Dublin suburb of Santry and concentrated on making munitions for the anti-Treaty IRA.

Pinkman continued to fight for the Free State, touring the south of the country to root out the Irregulars. In August he was in Cork, laying in wait to ambush de Valera. Acting on a tip-off, Pinkman and his colleagues were lying near a railway track outside Mallow, hoping de Valera would appear. 'I had no qualms about shooting Dev whom I believed to be so largely responsible not only for the outbreak of the Civil War, but also for its prolongation,' he said.[5] De Valera never appeared, but Pinkman's company stayed in the area to be inspected by Collins, who was on a trip to his native county from Dublin. Two days later it was Collins who was shot dead in an ambush at Beal na mBlath in west Cork.

Despite (or perhaps because of) dozens of books, hundreds of newspaper articles and several television documentaries dealing with the ambush at Beal na mBlath, no undisputed killer has emerged. Virtually everybody who was in involved in the ambush on the both sides has at one time or another been suggested as a possible assassin. There are over a dozen possible contenders for the man who shot Collins, including Glaswegian Free State Soldier Jock McPeak, who worked the machine gun on the armoured car in the Collins' convoy. The evidence against McPeak is flimsy and circumstantial, however, based on loyalty issues arising from his British Army background, eventual defection to the IRA and his Scottish birth.[6]

McPeak had joined the British Army in 1915 and been wounded at the Somme. He later served in Palestine, left the army in 1919 and returned to Glasgow, the city of his birth. McPeak's father was from Tyrone and when McPeak heard of the Black and Tan atrocities in Ireland, he became involved in gun-running for Irish republicans. Arrested and sent to prison in Scotland in early

1921 with 20 others, he remained there until the Treaty was signed. When the new Irish Army began enlisting in Scotland, McPeak joined. 'To us, it was still the IRA. We didn't know there was any difference at the time between them and the Free Staters. All we had been told was that they wanted soldiers,' he said.[7]

McPeak was given the job as gunner on top of an armoured car top with a machine gun called the Slieve na mBan. McPeak and the car were part of Collins' security convoy for the southern tour in August. After Collins' funeral McPeak returned to Cork and resumed as a gunner on the armoured car. Some days after the funeral he witnessed the murder of two IRA prisoners by Free State soldiers and – encouraged by two Cumann na mBan members he met in a pub in Cork – planned to desert. Three months after Collins was shot, McPeak defected to the IRA, and took the car with him.

He spent the winter, spring and summer on the run in Ireland before being smuggled back to Scotland in June 1923. Within weeks he had been arrested by local police and sent back to Cork to stand trial. He was released from Portlaoise Prison in 1928 after serving five years of a six-year sentence, and then he returned to Scotland. Still trying to escape his past, and inferences that he had been involved in Collins' assassination, he moved to England, changed his name, worked as a crane driver, married a second generation Irish woman, had two children, and died in 1974.

The immediate fallout from Collins' death shook Ireland. Joe Good, his friend from London, had refused to be drawn into the Civil War and resigned from the Free State Army at its outbreak. On hearing the news of Collins' death he immediately rejoined.

The pro-Treaty Free State forces eventually forced the IRA into submission, and the war was effectively ended by the spring of 1923. The end of the war saw Fitzgerald as Minister for External Affairs, de Valera and Markievicz imprisoned, and Childers dead, executed by the Free State in November 1922. Childers sparked so much bitterness in some of his Free State enemies that, according to information that surfaced towards the end of 2002, one of the soldiers present at his execution – a Lt.

Murtagh – reportedly rushed up to Childers' corpse as it lay in the coffin and fired a shot from his .45 Webley revolver into the dead man's face.[8]

While Pinkman resigned from the Free State Army soon after Collins' death in disgust at the torture of IRA prisoners, his enemy from the Moran's Hotel skirmish, Louis Noble, joined the Free State Army (without volunteering information about his anti-Treaty activities), and in April 1924 was made Instructor of Pipe Bands of the army.[9]

But the IRA did not die with the Civil War. A new generation of Republicans carried on the fight and, as before, some of the most influential figures in the movement were foreign-born and bred.

Seán MacBride had an odd mix of impeccable republican credentials and an unorthodox upbringing. His mother was Maud Gonne, a rich sophisticated woman who flitted on the European social scene in the early 1900s. Although born in England, she was taken with the romanticism of Irishman John MacBride fighting the British in the Boer War and – despite almost universal advice not to – married him in 1903.

Seán was born in Coleville, Normandy eleven months later, and less than four months after that his mother took him to be baptised in Dublin. The old Fenian, John O'Leary, was his godfather, although the priest refused to put O'Leary's name on the certificate as he was an agnostic. The boy was christened Seagan Gonne MacBride. His parents' marriage was already in trouble, and Maud Gonne started divorce proceedings in 1905. She won custody of her son and spoke only French to him, so that he would not be able to talk to his father.[10]

The hapless John MacBride returned to Dublin in 1906 but struggled to get work, until finally – in 1910 – he secured employment with Dublin Corporation as a water bailiff, getting dues from ships using the Liffey.

Seán remained in Paris and went to school, although his mother spent much time in Dublin campaigning for the Irish poor. In 1911, on a first communion souvenir, his surname is given as Gonne. In 1914 she took him to meet Padraig Pearse in Dublin with the intention of eventually enrolling him in Pearse's school, St Enda's. When he was 12 his father was executed for his part in the 1916 Rising. Although he had spent his first 14 years in France, and spoke with a French accent, his mother's contacts – and his father's republican reputation – assured his access to the highest levels of the republican movement. During the Treaty negotiations he travelled to London as an aide-de-camp to the Irish delegation and as a bodyguard for Collins, where he passed the hours playing bridge and chess.

His rejection of the Treaty led to a hard and bitter life in the IRA. The end of 1922 found him in Mountjoy Jail, sharing a cell with Rory O'Connor. Next door were two more leading republicans, Joe McKelvey and the Lancashire-born Liam Mellows. On the morning of Sunday December 8 all four were woken and told to dress. Then MacBride was left as the other three were taken away. Within hours he heard them being executed by a firing squad, in reprisal for a Free State TD killed the day before.

MacBride kept the IRA faith during the 1920s and into the 1930s. By then it was a demoralised and abject force, gutted by de Valera's successful move into constitutional politics and wearied by decades of fighting. Only the most intense remained to carry the torch. By 1936 MacBride had become Chief of Staff, chief custodian of the flame.

Yet MacBride's long years of service to the struggle did not ensure popularity in the ranks, and he remained an enigma to many of his men. 'Despite his 1916 name the average Volunteer felt MacBride was a strange Irishman: he had a peculiar accent, too much education and was very, very clever,' said one commentator. 'More than his politics within the Army or his plans for the future, it was his "differentness" which apparently grated, making him unpopular for a variety of often contradictory reasons.'[11]

One Sunday in Dublin in August 1936, while Chief of Staff, he was chairing a meeting of the Army Council. Detecting an undercurrent of tension he asked if there was a problem, and was told Kerry and Mayo were playing an All-Ireland football semi-final in Roscommon that afternoon and some of the members were keen to get away. 'So a game of football is more important than the future of the Irish Republic,' he burst out, flabbergasted, revealing a basic ignorance of his men.[12]

MacBride wanted to steer the movement towards a political programme, but his IRA colleague and rival Sean Russell urged mounting a bombing campaign in England. The two were locked in an intense struggle for the future of the IRA throughout the mid-1930s. For a while MacBride was ascendant, and during his time as Chief of Staff in 1936 had Russell court martialled for failing to account for money under his control. Russell was found guilty and expelled. But by the end of 1936, MacBride had stood down as Chief of Staff, Russell was back and plans for bombing England were under way.

MacBride soon drifted away from the IRA and into constitutional politics, though he continued to represent IRA defendants in his capacity as a barrister, and in 1972 offered advice to Provisional IRA Chief of Staff Sean MacStiofáin on how to handle face to face negotiations with the British government.

With MacBride out of the picture, Russell put his plan to bomb England into action. In early 1939, bombs exploded in cities across England, mass arrests were made, and a series of high-profile explosives trials took place with defendants of both Irish and English birth in the dock.

Ten IRA suspects were tried in Manchester. Only one, 30 year-old Joseph Broderick from Salford, was acquitted. 'Although of Irish descent,' said *The Times*, 'he was not a member of the IRA and had no political interest'.[13]

Less fortunate was 18 year-old Molly Gallagher from Islington, who appeared at the Old Bailey in April. Born and educated in London, Gallagher was charged with having potassium chlorate at her flat in Thornhill Square. Molly Gallagher denied any interest in the IRA, but police claimed to have found two rucksacks with potassium chlorate in them (each had seven 4lb packets) at her home on February 9.[14]

She was sent to Borstal for three years for her involvement with incendiary devices. Gallagher was treated separately from other defendants in a huge explosives trial that gripped the public imagination. There were so many accused – 22 men plus Gallagher – that the men were split into two groups and the dock for the accused had to be rebuilt. Evidence against her included Christmas cards from Peter Stuart, alias Peter Walsh, a co-accused in the trial. He refused to plead and was sentenced to 15 years after the judge described him as 'obviously one of the leaders of the conspiracy.' According to newspaper reports, the 25 year-old Walsh was 'born in Glasgow, the son of a pensioned police-constable in that city.'[15]

At the Walsh trial, an IRA memo 'to all unit commanders' was produced as evidence against the accused. It was, said the police, 'a description of how not to look like an Irishman – [with a] trenchcoat and hands in pockets etc…' and was presumably intended for first, rather than second, generation Volunteers.[16]

The 1939 campaign, and trials, threw up the question of IRA support among Irish communities in England and Scotland. How many Molly Gallaghers, dressing and sounding English, were lurking as fifth columnists, wondered the British public. Irish communities in England and Scotland were left uncomfortable and suspect. As C. Desmond Greaves explained, '[His friends] in the Labour movement did not understand that while most of the Irish in London were opposed to the bombs that threatened to bring a witch-hunt on them, they would think it unpatriotic to say so in the hearing of the English'.[17]

The Second World War meant that thousands of second generation Irish people joined the British military. Many, like Tony Northrop, served with great distinction. In the early years of the war Northrop operated behind enemy lines in Libya before joining the secret Special Operations Executive in 1943. He parachuted into southern Albania to assist the resistance guerrillas there.[18]

Others were heroes without leaving Britain. Several second generation Irishmen joined the British police and were awarded medals for their part in the war effort. PC Terence O'Connor of the Plymouth force was given the British Empire Medal for 'civilian bravery' as were Inspector Edward Gahan of the Metropolitan Police in London and War Reserve Constable Jerome Collins of the City of London Police. PC William Hannon of the Manchester Police also won the medal for helping to rescue a boy trapped in rubble. Hannon tunnelled his way through debris for two and a half hours to reach the boy, brought him to safety and then returned to duty, where he remained for 40 hours before collapsing.[19]

Other second generation Irish people were less inspired to help the British war effort. German radio used second generation Irishmen James Blair, William Joyce and Francis Stuart to broadcast radio propaganda. In early 1941, a memo was drawn up for the German Foreign Office by Adolf Mahr, who had lived in Ireland from 1927 until 1939. In 1934, the year after Mahr joined the Nazi Party, de Valera's cabinet appointed him Director of the National Museum in Dublin. During the war he was in Berlin, working at the Irish desk of the foreign ministry. He suggested in the memo that the Nazis ought to broadcast radio programmes to Ireland, and that second generation Irish people in Britain, the US and Australia should also be targets of German radio propaganda. He noted that 'at least one and a half million people living in Great Britain (London, Glasgow, Liverpool and many other centres, as well as being spread throughout the whole country) would be conscious of their Irish extraction…(all this without consideration of half-breeds totally absorbed in Anglo-Saxon culture)'.[20]

He expanded on the 'half-breed' theory: 'Approximately two-thirds of Irish descendants living in Great Britain might be caught up in Anglo-Saxon political ideology, but at least a third would have [Irish] nationalist sympathies,' he confidently declared. Mahr controlled German radio propaganda to Ireland from when it began in November 1941 until it ended during the very last days of the war, in May 1945.[21]

Several second generation Irish figures were recruited to make the broadcasts. British journalist James Blair had an Irish mother, and sometimes broadcast to Ireland under the name Pat O'Brien. Francis Stuart had been born in Australia and educated in England. He fought on the IRA's side in the Civil War and was married to Seán MacBride's sister Iseult. He did his bit for the German war effort in a series of broadcasts starting on St Patrick's Day 1942. The talks were primarily aimed at bolstering Irish neutrality, although Stuart also praised the IRA and advised his listeners in Ireland how to vote in the 1943 general election. Stuart presented radio programmes until early 1944, when he fell out with the station over his refusal to broadcast anti-Russian propaganda.[22]

William Joyce had been born in New York to an Irish father, was the most famous of all the broadcasters working for Germany, and was known in Britain as Lord Haw Haw. Highly valued by the German military, Joyce was awarded the Iron Cross by Hitler himself. Joyce was no lifelong Irish Republican, and had spent his teenage years in Galway as an informer for the Black and Tans. Joyce was captured soon after the war when a British soldier met him walking through a German forest and recognised his voice immediately. Joyce was tried and executed in January 1946.[23]

For many second generation Irish people the war offered a chance to prove their British credentials, an opportunity to lose their outsider status. But for others the 1939 IRA bombing campaign proved a more lasting influence on their identity. One London Irish schoolboy growing up in those years was to steer a radical change in the course of republican history.

6.

Seán MacStiofáin joins the IRA

It was a hot summer's day in Navan, Co. Meath on Monday May 21, 2001. More than 500 people crammed into St. Mary's Church for Seán MacStiofáin's funeral. Nearly all the benches were full long before the service began at 12.30 pm. Old men stood at the back – former IRA comrades and adversaries, the sweltering heat making their suits doubly uncomfortable. Sinn Féin President Gerry Adams arrived at 1 pm and sat near the front, his head buried in his hands in prayer.

Most of the funeral service was in Irish. There were a few brief mentions of MacStiofáin's 'public life', and references to his commitment to Irish language and culture and his support for the poor of Jamaica through religious missionaries. His childhood and early life went unmentioned, for they belonged to a different world.

MacStiofáin was born John Edward Drayton Stephenson in Leytonstone, east London, in February 1928. His father George was English, a Tory supporter complete with bowler hat. The young John Stephenson was very close to his mother, who was from Belfast. She had been married before, and had had three daughters much older than John. He was the only child from her second marriage. When he was about seven, she told him he was Irish, or at least half Irish, and not to forget it.[1]

The Stephensons moved several times around various parts of north London in John's early life. He went to a Catholic primary school in Islington where most of the children were from Irish or

Italian immigrant parents. He joined in on the Irish side during playground stand-offs, and spoke admiringly of the fact that the Italian kids had 'kept their language'.[2]

A few weeks before his eleventh birthday, his mother died. 'I was very close to her… I missed her badly,' he recalled. Eight months later, the week the Second World War began, he was evacuated from London with thousands of other children. First he was sent to Norfolk, and then six months later to Staffordshire, where he was housed with a mining family. They took him to see parts of Birmingham the German Luftwaffe had left as rubble, and he saw first-hand the devastation bombs could do to cities. He also witnessed what little damage the bombs had on British morale.[3]

When he was 14, in 1942, he reluctantly moved back to London to live with his father, who had remarried. The young John drifted from job to job and began to become increasingly interested in Ireland. He wasn't sure where this motivation came from – whether it was as a result of the IRA bombing campaign of the city, or simply 'something in my heart'. He began to go to local libraries and learn about Irish history. 'When I was about 15 I broke out crying at a book I was reading about famine in Ireland, and I said to myself one day I will work for Ireland,' he recalled. He bought a radio, and doggedly tuned into Radio Éireann's weak signal late at night, determined to listen until the Irish national anthem was played at closedown.[4]

He began to mix in Irish circles, and recalled being impressed by IRA medals belonging to a relative of London-Irish schoolmates. He went to the same haunts near Goodge Street underground station as Mike Brady in David Lodge's novel *Ginger, You're Barmy* and like Brady was conscripted into the British military for two years.[5]

He opted to join the RAF, and was enlisted in November 1945, at the age of 17. He got lucky, and was sent to a cushy posting in Jamaica, where he had an easy eight months running a small military clothing depot. His time in Jamaica appears to have been largely uneventful, although he claimed he did get into trouble for refusing to propose the King's health at a Christmas party. His remaining year back in the UK was even more unremarkable, pottering about in various RAF stations around the country. With only a month or so to go before discharge, however, he managed to wangle his way – against regulations – onto a special defence course, which gave him brief but intensive training into the use of a range of small arms weapons. He was already beginning to think about what might be useful in a future struggle for Ireland.[6]

Back in London as a civilian, he soon fell out with his father – 'a clever man who destroyed himself with drink, like his father before him,' he recalled. John Stephenson moved out into digs in Highgate and spent his social time on the London-Irish scene – at dances and céilís. He met and married Mary Casey, from Cork. He also joined the Anti-Partition League, and began to sell the republican *United Irishman* newspaper, but was disappointed that so few of his colleagues wanted to discuss revolutionary tactics.[7]

His restlessness for action led him to approach the few like-minded republicans in London with a view to forming their own IRA unit, based in the city. Contact was made with IRA HQ in Dublin, and Stephenson and five others were accepted on three months' probation as a unit. They were to gather intelligence on other international revolutionary organisations in an effort to pick up tips on guerrilla warfare. At the end of 1949 a letter on official IRA notepaper from Dublin confirmed the unit's status and Stephenson was appointed Officer Commanding (OC).[8]

It was not until the end of 1950 – when he had already been in the IRA for a year – that he made his first trip to Ireland. MacStiofáin was interviewed by RTÉ television in the early 1980s and asked 'did you think it was a bit crazy – fighting for a country you hadn't ever seen?'. He replied: 'I wouldn't say crazy. Maybe it was a bit strange. But I wasn't the first in Irish history to do that. Brian Ó h-Uiginn says in writing about 1916 a band of Volunteers came to Ireland from London, Liverpool and Glasgow to take part in the Rising. He says it was the first time many of them had been to Ireland. They came here to take part in the Easter Rising. Therefore, I'm not an exception.'[9]

Mystified by local Cork discussion of 'old time' and 'new time' (when clocks were altered by an hour for the summer months) he was also disappointed at the lack of republican fervour in his wife's community. Some locals sniggered at his patriotic ardour and he left saddened at 'the strange deadness in the national spirit'.[10]

Back in London, his enthusiasm undimmed, he joined the local Sinn Féin branch, started a republican paper and – on a hot night in August 1951 – painted *Roger Casement Died for Ireland 3.8.1916* on the wall of Pentonville Prison, where republican hero Casement had been executed and buried.[11]

At that time, he was living in Hornsey Road, north London. Below the doorbell outside his house he wrote both John Stephenson and – for the first time – Seán MacStiofáin. 'The first time Special Branch came to see me an Inspector wearing spats asked what it meant. It's my name in Irish, I said. "Oh," he said.' MacStiofáin's republican activities developed an increasingly military focus. He suggested to the Dublin IRA leadership that they invest in a new automatic rifle he'd heard about. Even in those early days, he claimed 'I believed that British government policy made inevitable armed struggle,' and that he ought to prepare himself for guerrilla warfare in the north of Ireland.[12]

In the summer of 1953, MacStiofáin received orders from Dublin to hire a van, get some wooden boxes made and find somewhere to store them. Later he was told he and others were to raid the armoury of the British officers' training corps in Felsted School, in Essex, not far from London. The others on the raid were Manus Canning, from the Derry unit of the IRA, and Cathal Goulding, a charismatic republican from Dublin. MacStiofáin had been chosen to go for his knowledge of the London area.

MacStiofáin planned to send the boxes of guns to Liverpool-born Séamus McCollum, the OC of the Liverpool IRA. The plan went well enough to begin with, with the men getting in through a window and piling the weapons into the van without much problem. On the road back, though, they were stopped near Bishop's Stortford by an eager young police constable for the minor offence of covering up the windows on the sides of the van, and their haul was discovered. It consisted of 98 rifles, eight Bren guns, ten Sten guns, mortars and magazines.[13]

At the police station the next day, an Inspector remarked on his accent but MacStiofáin and the others said very little in English. Although his knowledge of Irish was rudimentary at the time, MacStiofáin spoke it to the other IRA men in the station, and when they appeared before the magistrate's court a few days later all three answered 'Annseo' ('Present') when their names were called.

They were remanded in custody and sent to Brixton Prison in south London for three months before their trial. They expected to get about a ten, or possibly twelve-year sentence. At the trial, Goulding made the obligatory speech from the dock, declaring that 'only by force of arms can Ireland achieve her complete freedom…We have no apologies to offer'. MacStiofáin then stepped forward and said 'I am Irish by blood, descent and deliberate choice,' before associating himself with Goulding's statement.[14]

All three were found guilty, and all sentenced to eight years. They were put in the same van and driven to Pentonville Prison in Islington, near where MacStiofáin had grown up. But only Goulding was told to get out. When a warder nudged MacStiofáin and pointed to the Casement graffiti daubed on the wall, still there two years later, MacStiofáin didn't admit authorship. A Welsh warder in the van criticised MacStiofáin for being English in an Irish dispute, but the argument didn't last long as the van soon arrived in the west of the city, at Wormwood Scrubs Prison.[15]

The food was better in Wormwood Scrubs than in Brixton. MacStiofáin had been advised by Goulding – a veteran of detention – that if he kept himself and his cell clean and tidy he would be okay. MacStiofáin and Canning were in a different category to other prisoners, and seen as high-risk. They had to exercise separately and as they moved around the prison, to and from work, and had all of their movements recorded in a book. On their first night, an argument broke out between other prisoners about whether or not the IRA inmates should be regarded as enemies.[16]

MacStiofáin decided to concentrate on learning Irish – he took daily lessons from Canning – and to study the guerrilla campaigns in Algeria, Kenya, Cuba and elsewhere. The years passed predictably slowly, although Canning and he were eventually given an 'IRA table' outside the cells, and other unofficial privileges (including being allowed to read newspapers).[17]

Highlights included Canning's election to parliament in 1955 as MP for Derry, an unsuccessful escape attempt (when MacStiofáin tried to bribe a warder from Dundalk with £3,000 to help them get out), and in the summer of 1956 the arrival of six Cypriot paramilitary prisoners from Organosis Kyprion Agoniston National Organization (EOKA). The EOKA prisoners – whose number eventually grew to eighteen – proved invaluable to MacStiofáin's study of international guerrilla warfare.[18]

In October 1958 Goulding was transferred to Wormwood Scrubs to serve the rest of his sentence with his comrades. By then MacStiofáin's command of Irish was excellent and his Greek more than passable. In December that year MacStiofáin was briefly allowed out of prison to visit his wife, who had suddenly become ill after visiting him and was in hospital in London. 'It was very odd to see what had changed since 1953,' he said. 'Things looked flashier, and there were a lot of black people,' he recalled.[19]

MacStiofáin was released in February 1959, and within hours had left for Ireland, where his wife – now recovered – was living with their daughters. He was nervous that he might be rearrested when he got there, as Séamus McCollum had been after serving a sentence in England, but he was not. His welcome in Cork was very different now he was a republican hero – there was a torchlight procession headed by a couple of bands, and he made a speech to the crowd.[20]

By the end of 1959 MacStiofáin had found work for Gael Linn, the Irish language organisation, and his IRA responsibilities intensified. When the IRA border campaign – which had begun in 1956 and targeted border police stations and other installations – was called off in failure in 1962, MacStiofáin redoubled his republican efforts. That year, Seán Ó Ceallacháin became OC of the Cork IRA. 'Things were at a low ebb. The border campaign had gone badly, and when morale is low, revolutionary movements tend to fight among themselves,' he said. The Cork IRA, like other units, struggled with a right-left political tension. MacStiofáin was regarded as firmly on the right, and 'some of his views would be far removed from our socialist viewpoint,' said Ó Ceallacháin.[21]

Nonetheless, Ó Ceallacháin appointed MacStiofáin his Intelligence Officer. 'He kept an eye on all the Volunteers – you have to know what's happening. He'd let me know if anyone got out of line, and would keep an eye on police activity. Special Branch was forever trying to infiltrate our work,' he recalled. MacStiofáin – who didn't drink at that time – strongly disapproved of Volunteers drinking in pubs where the police would be listening out for loose talk, and introduced new rules about which premises Volunteers could frequent.

'I admired Seán immensely. The Volunteers appreciated he was a good soldier, knew what he was talking about and had the movement at heart. It's a pity we didn't have more like him,' said Ó Ceallacháin.

Despite his IRA work in Cork, he still regarded the north as the place for action. In the early 1960s he went there as often as he could – for holidays, weekends, any opportunity he could get. In July 1966 he and his family moved from Cork to Meath, much closer to the border. The aftermath of the border campaign meant an overhaul of the republican leadership. When MacStiofáin's comrade Cathal Goulding was made national leader he was pleased – he believed Goulding was a militant who understood the need for a vigorous military campaign.

But within a couple of years the IRA and wider republican movement revealed itself to be in identity crisis. A leftward shift in the leadership provoked disconcern and then alarm in many of its members. An effort in 1964 to end the policy of abstentionism – so that successful Sinn Féin election candidates would take their seats in Dublin, Westminster or Stormont and thereby recognise those parliaments – triggered a powerful reaction by traditionalists to hang onto one of their most sacred tenets. MacStiofáin was among those who opposed the reversal of policy, and his work in helping to defeat the reform offered him a prominent profile that resulted in his election to the national leadership.

In the following years, however, an obvious divide emerged between traditionalists like MacStiofáin and an increasingly Marxist-influenced faction within the IRA leadership. The leftists saw MacStiofáin and his supporters as too conservative, too Catholic, too narrow-minded in their pursuit of military objectives when a social and economic revolution, based on class, ought to be the IRA's focus. The left-dominated leadership accordingly put a low priority on arming the IRA, believing individual military operations to be secondary to wholesale street uprisings.

By the late 1960s, these tensions became increasingly fraught as the situation in the north deteriorated. The civil rights movement had led many Catholics to fear a Protestant backlash, and so for many northern republicans access to weapons became crucial. In this they were backed by MacStiofáin, who had for many years predicted and planned for guerrilla action in the north.

By the time a civil rights march was attacked by police in October 1968, and another in January 1969, the issue dominated IRA discussions – was it the IRA's role to arm Catholics in the north so they could defend themselves, or would that only fuel sectarian warfare and so retard the class-based revolution?

MacStiofáin had been on the IRA's Army Council for several years by then, regularly protesting to his boss, Cathal Goulding, about the IRA's leftward leanings. The rest of his efforts were spent as Chief of Intelligence, a post which meant he made frequent visits to the north to assess IRA strength. He soon won a reputation among northerners as a sympathetic ear from Dublin, one who understood that republicans desperately needed the weapons they were not being given by Dublin HQ.

During the mid-'60s the business relationship between Goulding and MacStiofáin steadily deteriorated. Goulding was impressed by left-wing thinker Roy Johnston, appointed to the IRA army council as director of education largely on the strength of having a PhD. MacStiofáin was dismayed.

Johnston did not introduce workers' revolutionary ideology to Irish republicans – there had been a healthy dollop of Marxism in the Citizen Army. MacStiofáin said that Goulding had mentioned to him as early as 1953 – when they were in prison together – that the IRA ought to make contact with Moscow, and indeed that when Goulding was appointed Chief of Staff he went to the Soviet embassy in London for help. Some even thought that the scholarly computer scientist Johnston was a Soviet agent sent to infiltrate the movement. Few believed this, but conservatives like MacStiofáin and Daithi Ó Connaill regarded his teachings as a sinister force, and suspected he wielded too much power over Goulding. 'He had a key weakness,' MacStiofáin said of Goulding, 'He felt inferior to somebody with a better education.'[22]

Johnston condemned the saying of the rosary at republican events as sectarian. MacStiofáin objected, and was suspended from the movement for two months. In an attempt to bridge the divide, MacStiofáin went to Goulding and said, 'Look, Cathal, we were once friends. I want to sit down and speak to you about the movement. You want the movement to be radical. I agree, but what about the military policy?' But MacStiofáin said Goulding replied 'No, that's out for the time being.'[23]

The bitterness grew personal. 'He's not the sort of fellow I'd look for after a political meeting to have a drink with,' Goulding said of the serious MacStiofáin, noting he was 'continually trying to prove he is much an Irishman as anyone else.'[24]

Although disillusioned with the IRA leadership, even with Goulding to whom he had once been so close, MacStiofáin could not bring himself to resign. By the summer of 1969 the possibility of large-scale violence in Derry during the middle of August looked real. The Apprentice Boys' march, held by Protestants, was due to take place on August 12 as part of the 'marching season'. It was rumoured that British troops or police might be sent to Northern Ireland if the local police could not cope. When Tuesday August 12 arrived, the Apprentice Boys' parade went off peaceably until the afternoon, when skirmishes broke out between those in the parade and Catholic youths from Derry's Bogside. The Bogside neighbourhood is an area of a few square miles, and for generations was almost exclusively Catholic. To keep Protestant attackers and the police out of the area, the Bogsiders had thrown up street barricades. Bogsiders threw stones across the barricades at the police, who responded with an occasional charge.

In Belfast, barricades were also put up around Catholic neighbourhoods to defend them against outside attack. Violence escalated throughout Northern Ireland. Full-scale rioting broke out in Derry that evening, and the Bogside was besieged by Protestants and an exhausted police force. Law and order collapsed as the rioting carried on non-stop for several days. Bernadette Devlin and other civil rights activists were in the Bogside breaking paving stones for ammunition to use against the police. Petrol bombs were also used against the police, and widespread sniping was reported from Belfast.

Irish Prime Minister Jack Lynch made a television appeal asking for UN troops to be sent to Northern Ireland to restore order. He moved Irish soldiers to the border to set up field hospitals for the casualties. In Belfast and in Derry local defence committees were hastily arranged to co-ordinate defence. Civil rights activists often took the lead in organising neighbourhoods. As far back as January, Derry civil rights leader John Hume had supported the formation of a local 'citizen's army' to defend the Bogside.[25]

Republicans – whether involved in the civil rights movement or not – became central to the defence of Catholic neighbourhoods, often with material support from the Dublin government. Catholics under attack looked to their traditional defenders – the IRA – for support, but the demilitarisation of the IRA in the mid-1960s had left them short of arms. In Belfast, Catholic streets were defenceless against attacks from loyalist mobs. The police proved unwilling or unable to prevent the violence, and so on August 15 the British government sent in soldiers to stop the rioting.

In the confusion over the role of defending Catholic neighbourhoods it is often difficult to distinguish those in the defence organisations from Republican groups. These allegiances were far from mutually exclusive, and it was common for people to be involved in both. What was clear, however, was that the republicans had lost ground in some Catholic neighbourhoods which had expected the Irish Republican Army – rather than the British Army – to protect them from the police and from loyalist gangs.

But not everyone involved in the IRA agreed this was their role. Francie Donnelly rejected the idea that the IRA was there to protect northern Catholics against Protestants: 'That's something that should be nailed, that the IRA existed solely to defend the Catholics in the north… the whole history of Republicanism… was not just as defenders of nationalists.'[26]

Predictably other republicans like Sean MacStiofáin disagreed. 'That was a looney attitude – the first function of any IRA unit in the north is to defend its people from attacks …' he said.[27]

And Ardoyne republican Martin Meehan noted that persuading people to join the IRA was, in the early days, done on the basis on defending neighbourhoods. 'First of all it was just on the basis of defence of the area. Defend your area and we'll make sure we back it up,' he said.[28]

In June 1969, Northern Ireland Civil Rights Association Chairman Frank Gogarty visited IRA headquarters in Dublin seeking assurances that civil rights activists would be protected by the IRA if the violence escalated, but he left unconvinced.

Republican strategists like Tomas MacGiolla saw the way forward for republicanism best served by a withdrawal of the IRA, rather than its resurgence. 'The objective was… to try and help the people defend the areas rather than have the IRA come out and start a new campaign. We never wanted the role of the defender of the Catholics,' he claimed. 'We wanted to avoid confrontation with Catholics and Protestants, but it developed from the Burntollet [January 1969 civil rights march] and I mean from that stage nearly every Protestant was on one side and every Catholic on the other side… it became sectarian in that way.' Despite the violence in the north, by the end of 1969 MacGiolla and the IRA leadership in Dublin were still trying to avoid a military campaign. 'That's why MacStiofáin was such an embarrassment,' he said. 'The objective was to avoid military confrontation and to avoid any appearance of sectarianism.'[29]

The IRA could not accommodate such contradictory approaches, and a split duly occurred in December 1969. A special convention of the IRA had been scheduled to vote on a proposal to end the policy of abstentionism and take seats, if elected, to parliaments in Stormont, Dublin and London. It was also to vote on joining a National Liberation Front with some far left groups. When the vote was taken, amid predictable charges of rigging, MacStiofáin and his supporters lost. According to one observer, MacStiofáin burst out at his former comrades 'You are no longer the IRA … we no longer regard you as such and we will take no further part in these deliberations.'[30]

7.
Provos March On

MacStiofáin and his supporters (about a dozen of the 50 or so delegates) left and began to form the new, Provisional IRA. A month later, in January 1970, the split was formalised when much the same scenario, if a little more dramatic, was played out at a Sinn Féin conference in Dublin. When a vote on abstentionism was put to the 250 Sinn Féin delegates, with the same result as the IRA verdict, MacStiofáin seized the microphone and led his supporters (about 80 of the delegates) out of the hall and into another, pre-booked venue.

When MacStiofáin was elected as the first Chief of Staff of the new, Provisional IRA, and the old IRA they had left became known as the Officials, the split was complete. For MacStiofáin, the difference between the Provisionals and the Officials was clear. 'The Officials say unless you have mass involvement of the people you haven't got a revolution. We say, the armed struggle comes first and then you politicise.'[1]

Some politicians in Dublin, apparently alarmed at the leftward lurch of the Official IRA, encouraged the split, and supplied the northern republican Provisionals with arms, training, and money. How much material support the Irish government delivered to the northern IRA units is hotly disputed; in 1970 the Irish Agriculture Minister, Neil Blaney, the Finance Minister (and later Taoiseach) Charlie Haughey, and an intelligence officer in the Irish Army, Captain James Kelly, stood trial in the Republic of Ireland for conspiracy to smuggle arms and ammunition to the north.

Although they were all acquitted, there is no doubt that the Dublin government tried to help Catholics defend their neighbourhoods from attack. Samuel Dowling, chairman of Newry and District Civil Rights Association, said he was supplied with gelignite, sub-machine guns and other arms by the Irish government to use for defending the Catholic population.[2]

MacStiofaín played down the Dublin government's role in creating the Provisional IRA.

> Most of the money [from Dublin] went to the defence committees in Belfast that were controlled by the IRA but the IRA got no arms or ammunition from the Dublin Government – maybe ten people went to a training camp from Derry. Those who got money were there as members of the defence committees…The scheme stopped a month after the [IRA] split, started again for six weeks and then stopped altogether. Some of the money went to the Sticks [Official IRA] before and after [the spilt].[3]

He denied that payments from the Dublin government to defence committees were, in reality, significantly subsidising the IRA, which used the money to pay their Volunteers. 'It was the responsibility of the [IRA] finance officer [to pay Volunteers]. Most would get £15, if married with children, £10 if married but no children, £5 if single. For a few weeks it saved us money [when the Dublin scheme was on] and I got two sums of £1,000 from [Republican Socialist Belfast MP Paddy] Kennedy. No training, no arms, nothing,' he insisted.

In his first year as Chief of Staff of the Provisionals, MacStiofáin believed the IRA London unit important enough to warrant several personal visits to the city. In the split of December 1969, MacStiofáin had the support of nine of the thirteen Belfast IRA units. Of the few units based in Britain, only London immediately went with MacStiofáin.[4]

He went three times in 1970, but had little time to visit his old haunts. 'I was in the west of London with Ruari Ó Braidaigh,' he recalled. 'He got lost – Ruari got lost after five minutes in Hammersmith market. After an hour, we went back to the house and found him.'

As 1970 drifted into 1971, MacStiofáin's IRA life became increasingly pressured.

> The weekend of internment [August 9, 1971] I went to Belfast one Friday with my wife and daughter. I had meetings with the brigade staff and meetings with battalion staffs and Saturday night I went to Derry, and ran into a roadblock… Joe Cahill was with me. We waited for 20 minutes and the officer shouted to another one 'Officer! This queue [at the roadblock] is too long. From this car' – and pointed at me – 'can go on'. Out of the window in my best British accent I said, 'Captain, you're a gentleman' and saluted.

It was a narrow escape, and the following months were spent in more meetings with IRA activists, scrutinising their plans and listening to demands for more weapons.

During 1971 MacStiofáin was in virtually constant contact with all the main IRA figures in the north. 'In the summer of '71 for at least 12 hours a day there were meetings, some days 16, 17 hours or more – meetings, inspection and camps,' he said. The format for OCs reporting to MacStiofáin followed a standard procedure. 'They would report if they wanted money, arms, training, anything. Then we'd discuss the next week plans for operations – they didn't tell me everything, but if there'd be an ambush, a mine or a boobytrap, or sabotage. The following week they'd tell me what happened.' His approach to leadership, he said, was 'learned from reading about Rommell's style – [go] right to the frontline and listen to the supporters' actions.'

Much of his time was spent deciding on what suggested operations would get the go-ahead. 'In practice it's the decision of the CS [Chief of Staff] to judge grey areas, usually after discussion with the Army Council but sometimes I would do things myself [make the judgement]. Somebody said, "Seán, you have a good policy that you take; a straight yes or no,"' he said.

He said he refused permission for many operations because of a risk to civilian casualties. 'No unit would use a car bomb unless it had specific instructions and permission from GHQ staff. Their operations officer had to get permission from OC in Belfast.' But a car bomb offered huge advantages, MacStiofáin saw, because it 'provided an efficient container and an efficient delivery system. It yielded far greater administrative, industrial and economic damage for a given operation. And it required fewer Volunteers to place it on target.'[5]

Many proposed attacks were turned down.

> In '71 someone told me [Lord Louis] Mountbatten comes here but the [IRA] Army Council said no action unless the situation becomes very bad, and then we'll send somebody to put a threat in the papers to warn him…'If Mountbatten continues to holiday in Donegal we would not be responsible for what happens.' That would've been enough. You can do things like that in a different way, there's no need to kill him. There was an IRA statement in Cork in 1964 that a British warship would have sailors attacked in Cork and the visit was cancelled.

In 1979, Lord Mountbatten, a prominent member of the British royal family, was killed by an IRA bomb while holidaying in Donegal.

One tactic MacStiofáin opposed, however, was bombing England. He was regularly pressured by IRA colleagues to allow attacks to be carried out on English cities, but he wanted to keep the option as a last resort. He reasoned that it would be too difficult to supervise an active IRA unit that was based in England (although 20 years earlier he had, of course, been keen to set up such a unit when he was living in London). The only killing he ordered in England was that of British Army General Frank Kitson.

Many civilians were killed by the IRA in Northern Ireland during MacStoifáin's time in charge. Months before he died, he explained his distinction between acceptable and unacceptable targets during those years.

> A suggestion to attack a big factory with loyalist workers was no. If sabotage, like on a post office or light or power installations, then okay. Attacks on RUC and British servicemen were okay. If you have a contractor building new barracks in my opinion the directors are legitimate targets. Every part-time member of the UDR had a pistol 24 hours a day and was on duty… there were two members of the UDR going to work together – one Catholic, one Protestant – and I said 'okay, do it' [attack them] and both were killed.

MacStiofáin claimed that he did worry about his victims. When he first ordered someone to be killed, he claimed he thought about their family. 'I said I hope they're not married, and then afterwards you'd say to yourself you must pray for their souls…'

The IRA attacks of 1971 seemed to bring a united Ireland no closer, but MacStiofáin and other top-level republican strategists appeared to have no new ideas to end partition. Then, in 1972, an offer of talks came from the British and an IRA ceasefire was announced. On July 7, MacStiofáin, Martin McGuinness, Gerry Adams, Ivor Bell, Séamus Twomey and Dáithí Ó Conaill met Northern Ireland Secretary William Whitelaw in a London house, on the north bank of the Thames. Before the meeting MacStiofáin sought advice from Seán MacBride. MacBride had accompanied Michael Collins to London for the fateful Treaty negotiations of 1921, was a former Chief of Staff of the IRA, and by 1972 an internationally-recognised lawyer prominent in Amnesty International.

> MacBride advised us not to interrupt when the British spoke and to sit together, not be separated in the seating arrangements. When we got in the room, Whitelaw gestured for us to sit here and there but I said no, we'll stay together.

MacStiofáin read a prepared statement, demanding the British declare their intention to withdraw from Northern Ireland on or before January 1, 1975. 'Only Whitelaw spoke for the British,' said MacStiofáin. 'We thought they'd refer our statement back to the cabinet and Whitelaw would take the statement to the Prime Minister'.

Frank Steele, an MI6 officer and part of the British delegation, was astounded by MacStiofáin's presentation. 'He behaved like Montgomery at Luneberg Heath telling the German generals what they should and shouldn't do if they wanted peace…', he recalled.[6]

The meeting produced nothing, although MacStiofáin anticipated it would be the first of a series ('Whitelaw had said leave it to our officials, yours and mine [to arrange],' he said). But there were to be no further meetings, and the lesson MacStiofáin said he took from the encounter was: 'Don't trust politicians'.

During the meeting, the groups broke to confer in separate rooms. 'Adams said "Maybe we'll get the declaration on intent [from the British to withdraw],"' recalled MacStiofáin. 'I said no, we must give them more stick and the casualties of the British Army after the truce were very high in my last six months as Chief of Staff. But we hoped that the truce would last.'

The truce only lasted for 48 hours after the meeting, and if MacStiofáin helped inflict high casualties on the British Army in the following months, the civilian population also suffered enormously.

Within weeks of the Whitelaw meeting, on Friday July 21 1972, the IRA planted and exploded 22 bombs in Belfast which, in just over an hour, killed nine people and seriously injured about 130 others. 'Bloody Friday' did serious damage to the IRA's credibility and to MacStiofáin's claims to avoid civilian casualties wherever possible.

In late November 1972, MacStiofáin was arrested in north Dublin, and given a six-month sentence. He immediately embarked on a hunger strike – standard procedure at the time. But, characteristically, he went further and also announced he was on a thirst strike. This infuriated some of his senior IRA colleagues, who had not approved such a move. It also dramatically shortened the window for negotiations. Although one might reasonably expect to last two months on hunger strike, life expectation on a thirst strike is only about two weeks. After eleven days he began to drink water, but still refused food. Huge demonstrations against his jailing took place in the north and south, with thousands of people cramming into Dublin's O'Connell Street to protest.[7]

In the first days of December, the *Irish Post* newspaper ('The Voice of the Irish in Britain') reported from Ireland that 'Sympathy with Sean MacStiofáin – the dying Provisional IRA leader – has grown considerably since the weekend. This is most discernable in rural areas. Protest meetings have taken place in many towns and thousands of signatures have been collected for petitions seeking his release.' It also suggested that 'the MacStiofáin affair provides a badly needed boost for the fortunes of the Provisionals and their political wing, Sinn Féin… If the Provisional and Sinn Féin leadership can now channel the new gush of sympathy, it may be in a position to demonstrate some worthwhile political muscle in the local elections due for next year.'[8]

As his health deteriorated, MacStiofáin was transferred to the Curragh military camp, and stayed on hunger strike until – 57 days later and 56 pounds lighter – ordered off it by the IRA Army Council. But MacStiofáin's star faded quickly, and he never regained his position at the top of the republican movement. Rumours were spread that he had asked to come off the hunger strike. Others quickly moved to fill the gap in leadership left by his imprisonment. Sidelined by the IRA, MacStiofáin remained publicly uncritical of his successors, but his influence had gone. For decades he remained in the shadows, an anonymous figure without too many close friends in the movement.

In 1986, he asked to see senior Sinn Féin official Pat Doherty, now a Sinn Féin MP for West Tyrone.

> He asked to see me because he did not agree with the decision made to do away with abstentionism. He was quite strong about abstention. He said, 'I don't agree with what's happened and you have no moral authority to do such a thing', and I said, 'Seán, whether you agree or not is irrelevant – we have every moral authority to take whatever

> decision we think is right.' We had a sharp exchange for a while but after that I got on very well with him.[9]

Occasionally, said MacStiofáin, he offered advice to the IRA leadership. 'In 1991 I was thinking to myself, well things can go on and on and on and I asked for a meeting with a member of the [Army] Council,' he recalled. 'I said, "Look, this period seems to me the same as '61 – if you continue like this you'll be isolated. I propose the army make a statement; the IRA will not engage in offensive action and if the British government and forces respond, maybe there will be a complete truce."'

MacStiofáin's place in the pantheon of republican – even Provisional IRA – heroes is strangely uncertain. Some regarded his hunger strike as a debacle, and found it hard to forgive him. 'Politics is hard, maybe republican politics would be tougher…' said Doherty of MacStiofáin's demise. A handful of former comrades remember him with real affection, but for the wider movement his reputation is that of an aloof, detached figure.[10]

His image has been damaged by British media perceptions, and was even attacked in fictional work. In Robin Moore's 1976 novel *The Kaufman Snatch* the reader is told that MacStiofáin had been 'deposed after losing face after an unquenchable desire for a cup of tea had led him to forget that he was supposed be fasting to death'. If that were not enough, MacStiofáin is further smeared when his successor as Chief of Staff accuses him of turning informer in a bid to get his clutches on a young female Volunteer. 'Few novels,' says Patrick Magee in his excellent survey of Troubles fiction, 'are as irredeemably as dreadful' as Moore's, but he was not the only writer to attack MacStiofáin.[11]

A front page story in the *Sunday Times* of May 5 1985 by Barrie Penrose headlined 'Provos' ex-chief was a police informer' accused MacStiofáin of being a police informer for nearly 20 years, citing anonymous Special Branch sources in Northern Ireland and the Republic. 'The officers say that MacStiofáin… had turned informer after the Garda had accumulated evidence – though not enough to prosecute –

implicating MacStiofáin in the death of an IRA renegade.' Penrose even claimed that police called MacStiofáin by his English name – 'Ah, John,' said one member of the Garda, 'he was a great friend of mine. I think he was doing it because he wanted to get rid of certain people.'[12]

Penrose's story recounts how – after confronting MacStiofáin with the allegations at MacStiofáin's house, he was unceremoniously ejected from the premises, and as he was driving away MacStiofáin hurled a car jack through the window of his car. Fifteen years later MacStiofáin could still recall the encounter with some relish.

The news of MacStiofáin's death brought predictably mixed judgements on his life. In Northern Ireland, *The Irish News* reported MacStiofáin's death by emphasising that both dissident and mainstream republicans joined in the tributes. It reported the funeral as 'Republicans united in grief'.

Sinn Féin leader Gerry Adams was among several hundred mourners at the funeral in the Republic yesterday of former IRA chief of staff Sean MacStiofáin... Other republican figures at yesterday's ceremony included Ruairi Ó Bradaigh, Gerry Adams's predecessor as Sinn Féin leader, who quit when the movement adopted a more political role in the mid-1980s.[13]

In a news piece for *The Independent* of London David McKittrick noted MacStiofáin's 'singular background,' and claimed MacStiofáin 'left a lasting mark not just on Northern Ireland's history but in its graveyards, where hundreds of headstones stand in mute testimony to his simplistic fanaticism'. The piece conceded that while the IRA was not responsible for all of the casualties of 1972, when almost 500 died, 'It was however responsible for a great many of them, killing 234 people in pursuit of MacStiofain's vain hopes of inflicting a military defeat on Britain.'[14]

As for MacStiofáin personally, it claimed

> the rest of the IRA, regarding him as something of an egomaniac, pushed him out early in 1973, leaving him with much time to brood on what he had done, and on the

> injustice he believed he had suffered at the hands of his former comrades. After a while he became something of a peacenik, occasionally calling for an IRA ceasefire. But he was a figure without influence, a historical curiosity from the frenzy of 1972, and for almost three decades he sat on the sidelines.[15]

Kim Sengupta, writing *The Independent's* formal obituary the following day, was more restrained, describing MacStiofáin as one of the IRA's more 'controversial and colourful characters'.

Further afield, both the *New York Times* and *Washington Post* carried obituaries of MacStiofáin, based on wire stories. 'A seasoned IRA activist even before the Northern Ireland conflict ignited in 1969, MacStiofáin was born John Stephenson in London and served in the British Royal Air Force,' explained Martin Cowley of Reuters in Belfast. 'MacStiofáin, whose mother was Irish and father was English, later adopted the Irish translation of his name but never lost his distinctive English accent during his time as a warlord in Ireland.'[16]

Although the Associated Press story included some minor mistakes (claiming MacStiofáin joined the IRA as a teenager, and that most of the IRA's weapons had been sold to Welsh nationalists in the 1960s) it also unearthed a quote it claimed was from Martin McGuinness about MacStiofáin: 'He thought everyone in Dublin should be dancing attendance on him. He served a purpose up until 1972, but it was clear by then he had no long term future in the movement.'[17]

Within days of his death attacks on MacStiofáin began in earnest, with claims resurfacing that he had acted as an informer for Garda Special Branch. The allegation, which appeared in Sunday newspapers in Ireland, claimed that he started to inform in the early 1970s, after being implicated in the murder and secret burial of a member of rival republican group Saor Eire. It was claimed there was insufficient evidence to convict him and so he was given assurances that he would not be questioned about the incident if he agreed to give information about the smaller group of dissidents. His information, claimed the newspaper reports, was apparently passed to the RUC and led to a number of arrests. It was claimed MacStiofain's handler was Hugh McNeilis, a Garda Special Branch officer who died in the 1990s.

The reports led to furious denials by Sinn Féin spokespeople, including Northern Ireland assembly member John Kelly, who said they were 'pure nonsense', and noted that similar stories had been circulated nearly 30 years before, and he blamed elements within the Official IRA for the smear campaign. 'When times were hard for northern nationalists it was he who made the break and came to the aid of northern nationalists, particularly those in Belfast,' said Kelly.[18]

The day after MacStiofáin died British journalist Simon Winchester told the Bloody Sunday Inquiry in Derry that he fled Dundalk in 1971 after MacStiofáin accused him of being a British army spy. Winchester was a reporter with *The Guardian* in the early 1970s. He told the inquest the incident happened when he was having lunch with Martin Meehan and several other high-ranking Provisionals in a Dundalk hotel.

'At this meeting they told me that they were being supplied with weapons by the general insurrectionary movement around the world and now had the materials to wage war,' he said. During the meeting, said Winchester, MacStiofáin telephoned the hotel and accused him of being a military spy, so Winchester hurriedly fled. He told the inquiry he did not 'see eye to eye' with MacStiofáin.[19]

The day after MacStiofáin was buried, a piece by columnist Kevin Myers appeared in the *Irish Times* which was more vitriolic than anything in the British press. Myers warned his readers to 'Beware the enthusiast from the margins of an identity who moves to the centre to redefine that identity. At its most extravagant, the phenomenon of the outsider seizing the centre is seen in the Austrian Adolf Hitler… and the Corsican Napoleon Bonaparte…, the Catholic Georgian Josef Stalin…' he wrote.[20]

> Seán MacStiofáin had barely a molecule of Irishness in him. He wished to bring civil war to a land he knew nothing about… Maybe that is the way of little corporals,

> a rank he had in common with Hitler and Bonaparte… He was such a mediocrity that you really must wonder at the culture which could accept him into its ranks and make him its leader…Was it his lack of regard for life or for any civilised values which gave him the edge in the competition for leadership of the Provisional IRA?[21]

Myer's attack, though extraordinary, was not unique. A month later, the 'Onlooker' columnist in the *Derry Journal* derided MacStiofáin for his accent and background, and criticised his performance in an RTE television interview that was recorded in the early 1980s and broadcast shortly after MacStiofáin's death.

'The interview with the former IRA chief-of-staff was conducted in Irish, and the combination of his English accent and eyepatch would have made for rather surreal television, except for the intrusion of the harsh realities of his actions,' it said. In fact, according to independent Irish language experts, MacStiofáin's Irish was fluent and although obviously not a native speaker, he did not have an English accent, but spoke with a hint of several regional Irish dialects (having learned his Irish first from Derry native Manus Canning while in Wormwood Scrubs, before living in Cork and then Meath). Nor was he wearing an eyepatch during the interview.[22]

Undeterred, the columnist suggested that 'One got the impression that he fancied himself as a revolutionary but did not have the moral fibre to make the ultimate sacrifice – one that he expected of his footsoldiers and one exacted on far too many innocent victims.'

It concluded with an observation about MacStiofáin's identity politics. 'It used to be said of Belfast loyalist Lenny Murphy that the embarrassment of having an Irish surname made him even more psychotic. One got the impression from the ex-RAF man, John Stephenson, whose father voted Tory, that he felt duty bound to be even more "patriotic" than the patriots.'

The piece triggered a furious response from Manus Canning, MacStiofáin's old prison colleague from the 1950s. 'I spent nearly six years in Seán MacStiofáin's company and I think I knew him fairly well. The Seán MacStiofáin I knew grew up in London and did his compulsory national service in the RAF. He had, naturally, an English accent but he mastered the Irish language in spite of the accent which offended "Onlooker,"' said Canning in a rebuttal printed in the *Derry Journal*.[23]

> Is there a single Irish family among the readers of the Journal which does not have a son, a brother, or a sister whose children are growing up in England, Canada, the US, Australia or elsewhere and picking up the accent they hear every day? Those children of the Irish Diaspora arrive in Derry every summer. They are proud of their Irish roots. Many of them play Gaelic football and learn the Irish language and Irish dancing. We must hope that they don't meet 'Onlooker'... Tom Clarke was born in the British army barracks at Hurst Castle in the Isle of Wight. James Connolly was born in Edinburgh. Edward de Valera, with a Spanish father was born in Manhattan and chose to be called Éamon de Valera in Ireland. Like de Valera, Erskine Childers, Jim Larkin and countless others, Seán 'chose the green' and, like many others, he paid a heavy price for that. Seán had a choice. Would 'Onlooker' have liked him better if he, 'John Stephenson' had joined the British army and arrived in Derry to make the croppies lie down. Many children of Irish parents did so and we did not love them for that.[24]

MacStiofáin was buried under the Meath sunshine in a grave surrounded by hundreds of wreaths, including one from EOKA. Ité Ní Chionnaith of the Irish cultural organisation Conradh na Gaelige gave the graveside oration, and although she spoke of MacStiofáin as 'one of the most important figures in Irish history, alongside of Pearse,' it was the blue flag of Conradh na Gaelige that draped his coffin, not the tricolour.

Had he died on hunger strike in 1973, perhaps his place in republican history would have been more celebrated but there was no regional constituency to argue for his memory, no plaque on his boyhood home in London, no volley of shots over his grave.

When Seán MacBride left the IRA in the late 1930s, his successors immediately began to direct a bombing campaign against English cities. MacBride had long opposed the tactic, but his departure meant the campaign could go ahead, and it started in 1939. As Chief of Staff, MacStiofáin had also vetoed bombing English cities, and his arrest and removal from the Provisional IRA leadership in 1972 in turn removed the last obstacle to the next republican bombing campaign in England.

8.
Second Generation Victims

MacStiofáin was arrested at the end of November 1972. Those in the IRA who wanted to bomb England wasted little time in taking advantage of his absence, and in March 1973 the IRA planted four car bombs in London, including one at the Old Bailey which killed one man and injured 180 other people.

By the following year IRA attacks in England were both routine and shocking. In February 1974 eleven people were killed when the IRA bombed a coach on the M62 carrying British Army personnel and their families. In October there were attacks on pubs in Guildford, in which five people were killed, and the following month in Birmingham, when 21 people were killed by two pub bombs.

Second generation Irish people were among the victims of the Birmingham attack. Two Birmingham brothers – 22 year-old Desmond and 23 year-old Eugene Reilly, whose parents were from Donegal, were killed in the explosions. John Reilly, the brothers' father, was called by police to a mortuary to identify the body of one of his sons. The *Irish Post* reported:

> He believed that the body would be that of Eugene and that his other son Desmond was 200 miles away in Durham.

> But the two brothers had been having a reunion drink in the Tavern in the Town [pub] when the bomb exploded and a heartbroken John Reilly had to identify the first body as that of Desmond. He was called again to the mortuary by police and found the body of Eugene.[1]

Other mourners included the Irish father of Anne Hughes – a Birmingham Irish girl who had been having a drink after work with a friend. Both girls died in the Tavern in the Town. 'There was just one body left and the police said would I like to see it', said Mr Hughes, who lived in Sutton Coldfield. 'It was Anne. The whole thing is tragic. There is no sense in what has happened,' he told the *Irish Post*.

An estimated 35 of the nearly 200 injured were also Irish. They included 20 year-old junior solicitor Peter Long, whose father was from Cork. He was in the Mulberry Bush pub and suffered neck injuries in the blast.

Bernadette O'Connor, aged 17, whose parents were from Athlone and Kerry, was walking up the stairs from the Tavern in the Town when the bomb went off. She suffered severe burns to her face and legs and head injuries. She worked locally as a shop assistant, as did Yvonne Donnelly, also 17, whose parents came from Kildare and Laois. She suffered severe face and leg burns as well as other injuries. Anthony Fleming, aged 20, whose parents were from Galway and Kilkenny, was walking past the Mulberry Bush pub when the bomb inside went off. He was knocked unconscious, thrown across the street and woke up in hospital suffering from shock and severe facial lacerations.

These pub bombings, and dozens of others in 1973 and 1974, left Irish communities open to suspicion, and attack. In the days after the Birmingham bombs, Prime Minister Harold Wilson made a plea for no acts of retaliation against Irish people or people of Irish descent, and Home Secretary Roy Jenkins warned in Birmingham the day after the bombings that nothing would be worse than an attempt to take it out on people of Irish origin. These calls went unheeded. Within hours of the Birmingham pub explosions bombs were thrown into an Irish-run Prince of Wales pub in Ealing's Boston Road, an Irish tobacconist's in Streatham, south London, and an Irish pub in Kingstanding in Birmingham. The Irish Community Centre at Digbeth was petrol bombed, and St Gerard's Catholic School in Castle Vale was hit by an arson attack. Workers at Liverpool and Manchester airports refused to handle flights bound for Belfast or Dublin.[2]

Kevin Barry Curran, a second generation Irishman from London, is the current Secretary General of the huge GMB union in Britain. At the time of the pub bombings, he was working in Birmingham. 'We were all in digs and there were some apprentices from the loyalist community and I told them not to go out that night. But they argued that the IRA was nothing to do with them. I said that once people heard their accents they wouldn't understand the difference – as far as anyone is concerned, you're Irish,' he told them. The young Protestants ignored Curran's advice, went out, and were beaten up.[3]

'The disastrous bomb outrage in Birmingham did the Irish movement in Britain more harm than a regiment of cavalry,' said C. Desmond Greaves.[4]

Clare Short, former British Secretary of State for International Development, was born and brought up in Birmingham. Her mother's family is called O'Loughlin and has Irish roots from a few generations back. Her father was from Crossmaglen in south Armagh. On the night of the Birmingham pub bombs the Short family was particularly alarmed, as Clare herself later recalled.

> We thought that night that one of my brothers was in that pub, so the very first thing was we thought he might be hurt, and then he came home very late – he'd been somewhere else. It was a truly awful business with bits of people's bodies being collected in the street and so on and of course a lot of people in that pub were of Irish origin. Birmingham is a city with a large population of Irish origin and then this nasty atmosphere grew up in the city [after the bombings]. There'd always been a St. Patrick's

> Day parade since I was little – we'd all gone on it – and it stopped. There was this sense of Irishness being connected with this horrible evil thing.[5]

Short had a highly developed sense of Irishness by the time of the bombing.

> We were brought up very strongly in the sense of our Irishness. I went to Irish classes and got my medals and we went to Irish language classes and learned our prayers in Irish and we were brought up to believe that British imperialism was deeply evil,' she said. 'Ireland seemed wonderful and romantic. And you know how you grow up with that sense of it's a perfect place, and everybody is perfect and they all believe in justice unlike the terrible wicked British who've done awful things in the world. When you're a child these things are simple…then you grow up and nobody's perfect,' she said.

Birmingham in the mid-70s was not an easy place to be identified as Irish.

> Some of my cousins with the O'Loughlin name said they got rude remarks on the bus and so on and there were fights in pubs. Then of course not long after the story [surfaced] that the wrong people had been arrested [for the Birmingham bombings]… and my father went with one of my sisters to some of the trial and we already had this whisper [about the wrongful arrests]. That became the great thing – if you said these might not be the right people it was like you were guilty of the bombing, and I can remember when I first became an MP I gave an interview and said you know, there are reasons to worry that the wrong people had been convicted and that was just read as you saying 'it is a good thing to have bombs'. It seems extraordinary now but anyone then who questioned who'd been convicted was seen as somehow excusing the bombing so that very quickly became the story, the issue. My dad had a friend who used to come

> regularly who got involved in the very early campaign… to question the convictions and he went sort of creeping around worried that people were following him, and they probably were.

The St. Patrick's Day parade has been reinstated in Birmingham but during the 1970s Irish communities in Britain came under huge pressure to publicly renounce the IRA, or risk suspicion.

Journalist and author Blake Morrison was born in the north of England to an Irish mother and English father. His mother downplayed her Irishness, and had little contact with her family in Kerry. Morrison was living as a student in London when the IRA bombed the city in the 1970s, but suggested that any understanding he had for the campaign did not necessarily come from his mother. 'I remember walking past post boxes with a kind of trepidation because there was a time when bombs were put in central London post boxes and I walked past a lot of those, so of course I was conscious of it,' he said.

> [I thought] …Yeh, I understand how these people [the IRA] have been driven to this and I as a Brit and the country I belong to are guilty here – our hands aren't clean. We're not just victims of terrorism, there's a history here. I don't think my mother encouraged that or implanted that in me at all.[6]

Mark Wogan, son of broadcaster Terry Wogan, was born in west London, grew up in the city during the 1970s, and firmly identifies himself as Irish.

> I consider myself Irish. Definitely. I still hold an Irish passport, I don't hold an English passport. Never have. I'm an Irish citizen as much as anyone else. Both my parents are Irish – we behave in a very Irish way. My friends probably see me as English but it's not something we discuss. Inside I'd say I'm Irish… My brother and sister would definitely say the same – definitely say that they feel Irish…There's so much to being Irish that's to be

proud of and to celebrate.[7]

Wogan remembers the dark years of being Irish in England. 'During the 70s if you were Irish everyone thought you had a gun and were going to blow them up and maybe throw a petrol bomb at them and it didn't matter where you were from in Ireland, you were Irish and therefore a terrorist.'

After the pub bombings the British government rammed through the *Prevention of Terrorism Act* (PTA), aimed at rooting out terrorists in the Irish community in Britain. The legislation bore all the hallmarks of a rush job – denying fundamental safeguards and targeting people on the basis of their ethnic identity. As Paddy Hillyard pointed out in his landmark study of the PTA, it allows people to be arrested where no actual offence has been committed and where the person is not suspected of committing any offence. Random investigations are allowed under the PTA. Police still don't even have to suspect that someone has information, only that they belong to a category (ie they're Irish). In fact, one senior policeman told the *Mail on Sunday* that people ought to report Irish neighbours so that police could 'check them out'.[8]

In the early 1970s several organisations were established in Britain in response to the Troubles, including the Anti-Internment League, Troops Out and Provisional Sinn Féin. Many second generation Irish people were active in the Connolly Association, set up in London in December 1938 as the Connolly Club by left-wing Irish republicans. The organisation had two main aims: firstly to promote socialism (and particularly the teachings of James Connolly) amongst the Irish in Britain; and secondly to raise the question of the partition of Ireland and the nature of the repressive unionist regime in the north of Ireland. The Association was never a mass movement but the influx of Irish workers into Britain did give it a degree of influence in the British trade union movement, and it developed early links with the civil rights movement in Northern Ireland. But the 1973 and 1974 bombs in England, and the subsequent introduction of the *Prevention of Terrorism Act*, ended much Irish political activity as police conducted hundreds of raids on Irish homes in England and Scotland.

Margaret Brady, born in Glasgow of Irish parents, was one of the first questioned under the new PTA. Although she grew up in a house where her parents spoke Irish and as a young girl was an enthusiastic Irish dancer, she was not involved in Irish political affairs. 'I got a British passport to go to Majorca when I was about 19 or 20. There was no issue about it at all,' she said.[9]

In the autumn of 1974 she worked part-time in an antique furniture shop in Glasgow. 'I went to open the shop and I had my son in a nursery school locally. I went to open the shutters and there were two men, one either side of me and they ordered me into the back,' she said. 'They might have said they were Special Branch – I knew they were so they must have said it.' Although her questioning was relatively short, and by comparison with others who were detained fairly light, the experience was intimidating enough.

> They took me into the back shop. One of them had one of those Sherlock Holmes pipes. In the back shop we had racks of books… I remember the one with the pipe was looking through them and the other one was asking me my name and saying, 'Look, if you don't give us any information we're going to hold you up to seven days under the PTA.'

The police were apparently more interested in a republican workmate of Brady's and questioned her intensely about him. 'I was thinking my God, who's going to get my son at nursery because he used to be picked up at 12 o'clock and this was maybe half past nine in the morning,' she said.

The police left soon afterwards, and Brady was not even asked to accompany them to the station. Nonetheless, the experience was a traumatic one and raised issues for her about her Irish identity. Brady's son went on to play football for Ireland at under-21 level. 'It was through me, not through his father [that he qualified to play for Ireland],' she said.

Others were not as fortunate as Margaret Brady. For some people, questioning under the PTA led to many years in prison for crimes they did not commit. Six Irishmen from Birmingham – Paddy Hill, Dick McIlkenny, Hugh Callaghan, John Walker, Gerry Hunter and Billy Power – were wrongly convicted of the city's pub bombings. Two more Irishmen living in London – Paul Hill and Patrick Armstrong – were wrongly convicted of the Woolwich bombings. Hill, Armstrong and another Irishman, Gerry Conlon, were wrongly convicted of the Guildford bombings, as was an English girl, Carole Richardson, whose guilt by association as Armstrong's girlfriend was enough to condemn her. After severe physical abuse by Guildford police, Hill and Conlon named Conlon's aunt, Anne Maguire, as an accomplice. Although completely innocent, her home was raided in December 1974 and she, her husband, three of her children and three others were arrested. The three children – Vince, aged 16, John, 15 and Pat, 13 – had Cockney accents and there was some confusion among the police over the boys' nationality.

The family was an unlikely target. Although Catholics from Belfast, Anne and her husband Paddy were not involved in republicanism in any way. Paddy was a former member of the British Army, and proud of it. He was seen regularly drinking in the local British Legion club in north London. The Maguires had a bust of Winston Churchill on display in their house in tribute to the war leader. Paddy hoped his eldest son Vince might follow his example and join the British Army, maybe even go to the officer training college at Sandhurst. It was the youngest, Pat, who wanted to be a soldier, though, and had collected toy models of every regiment of the army. Vince had other ambitions.

> I wanted to be a copper. I went for the interview and everything – did the aptitude test. I used to watch The Special Branch on the telly and The Sweeny and all that and because they were always ducking and diving, always up to something, I wanted to do what they were doing – running round in Jags and 'You're nicked' and 'Shut it!' and I thought that'd be great.[10]

Although the boys had heard about the Troubles, and on their regular summers with relatives in Belfast even seen British soldiers, it had little daily impact on their London lives before December 1974. 'My dad was passionately British at that time – very, very proud of being a soldier and being British,' said Vince. He insisted that the boys not be sent to Catholic schools in London, and unlike many second generation children they were not encouraged to take part in Irish activities. 'I know now there were kids of my generation who went to play Gaelic football or joined Irish societies, but I wasn't aware of it then,' said Vince.

> The only Irish culture we had was records, Irish songs. I used to know every single rebel song by heart, like Kevin Barry. At that time such records were not seen as suspicious and were openly promoted through popular high street shops. They used to sell them in Woolworth's for God's sake, in a little hat stand thing that spun around. I used to know all them but I used to know all the Protestant songs because my dad had The Sash [My Father Wore] – he used to like putting that on at a party to wind the rest of them up.

Unsurprisingly, as a child Vince Maguire had little understanding of the divisions in Belfast. 'When we were kids we used to think Georgie Best was our uncle because he was one of the few people we used to hear talking with a Belfast accent and I remember going round telling people Georgie Best is my uncle when was I was seven or eight years of age,' he said.

At about that time, in 1966, England reached the final of the World Cup, where they played West Germany. Vince was on the usual summer trip to see his Belfast relatives when the match was on.

> I remember in my mum's mother's street there were two TVs – one of them happened to be in the next door neighbour's, next to where we lived and it was packed with people watching it. I remember walking into this room and I shouted 'England!' or 'Come on, England' and was told, 'Get out you little fucker', you know. [They

> were shouting] 'Come on, Germany, come on, Germany' and I remember turning to one of my aunts and saying, 'Why are they cheering for Germany? Why aren't they cheering for England?'

The boys had no allegiance to the IRA. Pat recalled how exciting it was to see British soldiers in Belfast. 'For me seeing the army was like, "Yeh, lovely, that's what I want to do". I remember one time being with a group out throwing stones at the jeeps and one of the bigger kids said you have to throw them [and gave me a stone] and I had to – and missed,' he said.[11]

The middle Maguire son, John, also recalled the visits to Northern Ireland, the sight of British soldiers, and the boys' disinterest in politics.

> The only way we knew Belfast existed was because that was our summer holiday. My mates were going to Benidorm, we were going to fucking Belfast… I remember as kids… a bit of peer pressure [to join the stonethrowing at British soldiers]. You can't be Billy No-Mates standing back there. You just went along with it as kids. Nothing malicious – no petrol bombs. It was fun, exciting, then getting chased by the soldiers, turning round and shouting 'Aaah, British bastards' and then thinking about it afterwards…[12]

The innocence ended on December 3, 1974, when the police arrested the boys and their parents. Anne Magurie, their mother, said she 'snapped and became hysterical' when a policeman told her the boys were being taken to the police station. 'I told him to leave them alone, that they were English born and bred.' (In fact Pat had been born in Belfast in March 1961 during a trip home to see her family.)[13]

A policewoman talking to the boys in the house asked 'Are you English or Irish?', to which Pat replied, 'Oh that's it, is it? You think we're bombers?' Down at the police station Detective Sergeant Hunt asked Patrick why he thought the police had raided their house. 'Because we're Irish I suppose,' replied the boy.[14]

Patrick was not far wrong. The London police who arrested the Maguires had apparently been told by their colleagues in Guildford they would be arresting hard-core IRA operatives. At the police station, 15 year-old John was accused of being an IRA sleeper. 'They kept saying to me "All right Paddy?" and I was saying "Hold on, my name's John". They said, "You've just been planted in London [to do IRA work]." I said, "What do you mean, planted? I live here! Where do you think I was planted from?",' he said. 'They asked about Irish people we knew. We knew mum and dad but weren't even sure if dad was proper Irish – he was in the British Army. We weren't 100 per cent sure if dad was proper Irish.'[15]

Meanwhile, 13 year-old Pat was being questioned about his republican politics.

One of the questions I was asked was if I knew what the colours of the tricolour were and I said, 'I don't know what you're talking about'. If he'd said the Irish flag I would've said, 'Green, white and gold', but I didn't know what he was talking about and he thought I was talking the piss. I just didn't have the knowledge about it.'[16]

Despite their protest, and despite the lack of evidence against them, Vince and Pat Maguire, their parents and three others were convicted of terrorist offences which they had not only not committed, but which had never taken place. None of the Maguires made any confession, despite severe physical abuse. 'Why did they beat up a thirteen year-old like Patrick – surely the only child detained, beaten up and imprisoned under the *Prevention of Terrorism Act* in mainland Britain? I will never understand that,' said his mother.[17]

The police alleged that just before they raided the house in north London the family, plus some hangers-on, had been up to their elbows in bomb-making equipment. No explosives were ever found in or anywhere near the house. The evidence against the Maguires amounted to those parts of Hill's and Conlon's beaten confessions which mentioned Anne Maguire, and some totally discredited forensic science which suggested some of the family had been handling explosives just before the police came in.

After the three boys were first arrested in December 1974 they were released, then Vince and Pat were rearrested nearly three months later and charged with possession of explosives. Vince tells the story.

> It was two reporters who told me I was going to be charged. I remember them coming round one weeknight… they said, 'Does anyone fancy going out for something to eat?'…We went to a restaurant in Queensway, and we were having a Greek meal and they said to me, 'By the way, we've heard it on good authority that you and Pat are going to be charged with possession of explosives'. I remember going down to the toilets – I'd had a drop of wine, and I chucked my ringer up, through fear. I always remember to this day being scared because up to then I hadn't been. I'd just gone along because all I'd got from my mum and dad was just keep strong, keep yourself together – it's all a mistake, you know we've got nothing to do with it. We'll all be out soon. We always believed we'd never be put away – how can they put innocent people away?[18]

Oddly, the middle son – John – was not charged. Pat and John now believe that the police simply made an administrative blunder, and intended to let Pat go because he was the youngest, but let John go instead. 'We're very similar in height. I'm Patrick Joseph and he's John Patrick,' said Pat. 'People say I look younger than Pat and they always thought I was the youngest boy,' recalled John. The mix-up cost Pat a four-year prison sentence.[19]

People who knew the Maguires were astonished by the arrests. Some people avoided them out of suspicion and fear, lest they be guilty by association. Vince recalled:

> A lot of the neighbours shunned us straight away and that hurt big time. People who we thought were friends. And people who we didn't know were our friends became our

> friends and stood by us, acquaintances who stood by us, like Mister Atkinson – he fought tooth and nail to try and prove our innocence, born and bred stonewaller Englishman, no Irish in him whatsoever. He stood by us, and lots of Irish people [didn't]. I know now a lot of it was from fear and ignorance. A friend of ours went out to his garden and buried anything to do with Ireland – records, everything, in the garden in case the police came and gave his place a spin. He was second generation, same as us.[20]

Despite enormous evidence pointing to their innocence from the earliest days after their arrest, no one inside the criminal justice system came to their aid. 'You hope you've got a copper there who's got brains who says, "No, that's bollocks!" but there was no one there who said that and why would there be?' said Vince. 'They're all looking out for promotion, they're all looking after their own backs. You can imagine what pressure them coppers [in Guildford] are under.'[21]

John Maguire agreed: 'There was a lot of coppers there who knew [the truth] but what could they do? You had the head of the bomb squad saying this woman blew up so and so. What's some rookie cop going to do? Say, "No, I think you're wrong commander"?'[22]

What happened to the Maguires could have happened to any of thousands of Irish families living in Britain in the mid-1970s. At their trial at the Old Bailey in early 1976 their parents were each sentenced to 14 years in prison, the eldest boy Vince to five years and Pat, the youngest, to four for possession of nitro-glycerine. Giuseppe Conlon, Sean Smyth and Pat O'Neill were given 12 years each. Giuseppe Conlon was to die in prison within four years. John recalls:

> I remember the last day, the morning of the sentencing. One of the neighbours came up to my mum and gave her a piece of coal. Apparently it's a symbol of good luck. I'd never heard of it. My mum's going to the Old Bailey, charged with terrorist offences, with this lump of non-specific black stuff in her hand…[23]

When the Maguires were declared guilty by the jury, the judge turned to the boys and said: 'It is only for you two that a vestige of real excuse can be found. I can appreciate that your position was one of great difficulty, but you must have known the gravity of these offences.' He explained he would show them no leniency because 'At the present time there is an obvious danger that any mercy extended to two boys on the grounds of youth will encourage the use of other young people.'[24]

The Times reporter Chris Borrell profiled the boys' mother. 'The jury could not fail to be impressed with the outwardly simple, homespun manner in which she gave evidence,' he said, but despite this he noted that 'Members of Scotland Yard's anti-terrorist squad are convinced that Mrs Maguire was a vitally important cog in the Provisional IRA network operating in London'.[25]

John was devastated by the sentence handed to his mother. 'I was watching it on the evening news,' he said. 'To me, I was 16, and 14 years was a lifetime. And [my sister] Anne-Marie was in the back room, and she was only seven years of age. She went mental. Then I had a woman come to the door who owned a second hand shop on the Harrow Road. [The news announcing the sentences] had only been on the telly an hour before. She said, "I'm ever so sorry to hear about your mum but obviously you'll be selling up and I'll do you a good deal." That was in less than an hour,' he said.[26]

9.

The Unusual Suspects

Vince and Pat Maguire spent the next few years trying to cope as prisoners, knowing that their parents, also innocent, were in prison too. When Pat was first sent to jail he was put in a room with other prisoners while officials busied themselves outside filling in forms and processing the new arrivals.

> I was sitting there chatting with this [London] accent and someone's gone, 'There's an IRA geezer coming in here, a young fella from the Old Bailey' and he's telling this story and I'm going, 'Oh yeah?' and all of a sudden they called my name out… that broke the ice. The first night I got in the cell very late and the fella in the next cell was from Belfast and he got up and [in a shouted whisper], 'Paddy, all right?' I've jumped up and had half an hour talking to him in a Belfast accent so he didn't think he had the wrong bloke. In the morning he came into my cell and said, 'All right'. I've gone, 'Yeah, I'm all right, mate' [with my normal London voice]. That confused a lot of people, the accent.[1]

Vince was sent to Wormwood Scrubs prison in west London.

> You've got to imagine how your mind's going when you're first put away. You're well pissed off to put it

> mildly. They sent in governors and assistant governors to assess my mental state and I said I've got nothing to do with the IRA, I hate the IRA, what they do to people, kill people, kill innocent people, I don't believe in anything like that, it's a big mistake [that I'm here]. About a week or so later they said we might have a bit of a problem – we've got an IRA prisoner who's proud of being [in the] IRA coming on to the landing – are you going to cause a problem with him? I said no, as long as he doesn't give me any trouble. He came in, he was Paul Norney, and he was like the build of a 10 or 12 year-old child. Slim, elfin-faced, long hair, had an escapee's patches hanging off him – miles too big for him and I saw him and thought, 'My God, is that the IRA?' I'd never met anyone in the IRA before in my life. We talked and he didn't say I know you're innocent, but he said, 'Look, I know you're not IRA. I'd know.'[2]

Norney was to become one of the longest-serving republican prisoners – aged 17 when he was arrested in Manchester in July 1975, he spent over 20 years in jail.

A few months before the Maguires were sent to prison, police in London cornered a group of IRA men in the city's west end in a house in Balcombe Street. The men, including Glaswegian Hugh Doherty, surrendered after a prolonged and highly-publicised siege in December 1975. By the time they were tried it was January 1977. Some of the 'Balcombe Street gang' as they became known, insisted they had carried out the bombings at Guildford and Woolwich, and that the Guildford Four were innocent. This had huge implications for the Maguires, for if the Guildford Four were shown to be falsely convicted, it raised serious questions about the evidence against the Maguires. Despite the admissions by the IRA men, both the Maguires and the Guildford Four were unsuccessful at the Court of Appeal.

Vince and Pat were put in separate prisons, but were brought together to be taken for visits to see their parents in jails elsewhere. 'Once we were in the Scrubs waiting for an escort to take us to see my mum,' recalled Pat. 'We were in there for two weeks I think and the first Sunday in church the Balcombe Street gang were there and other IRA fellas. As we walked in they stood up and one of them came over and apologised on behalf of the IRA "and while you're here," he said "you'll be alright, no-one will bother you."'

Vince explained the power of the IRA in prisons at that time. 'The IRA take over the nick if there's enough of them in there. They run the place,' he said. 'None of this gangsters running it – [the IRA are] in a different league. I've no admiration for them but they're in a different league – it's a different game altogether.'

While the two teenagers tried to adapt to prison life, their brother John and little sister Anne-Marie were taken in by relatives and tried to grow up as normally as possible. As Vince recounted:

> I think John would rather have done bird to be honest. He was on the outside and he had to deal with all the crap when we were put inside... They heard all these stories about prison, all exaggerated. It was quite a strict regime – there were things going on but nothing serious. They were seeing all these American films with prison gangbangs and drugs all that and were thinking what's going on? And they had to put up with all the snide remarks outside.

There was more for the young John and Anne-Marie to cope with in the aftermath of the publicity around the sentencing. 'I was taking Anne-Marie to school and someone came up to me on the Harrow Road and spat in my face,' recalled John. 'I went to live in Belfast for a while. It was a question of having to.'[3]

John and Anne-Marie stayed with relatives in Belfast and tried to adapt. 'Anne-Marie went to stay with my aunt Mary, my mum's sister, and I went to stay with my granddad,' said John. One night, someone from the IRA 'knocked on the door, and they said there's an envelope there for the boy. My granddad said he doesn't want it, we don't want it. Get away from the door. They came around once and that was it. It was IRA money.'

John's second generation status proved as difficult an identity in Belfast as it had been in London for the teenager. 'I couldn't win,' he said. 'In those days I'd walk down the Harrow Road and barrow boys who knew me wouldn't look at me, or if they did they called me an Irish cunt. That's one of the reasons I left [for Belfast]. Then when I got to Belfast people said, "Aah, you English wanker". And I thought, what can I do to appease these people?' The 16 year-old worked in a stables in Black Mountain and tried to avoid trouble. 'It was a funny experience in Belfast because I was known as a Brit… because of my accent. The British Army obviously knew who I was so [to them] I was an IRA cunt. They knew exactly who I was. I got aggro out there,' he said. After 14 months he left Belfast and returned to London, taking young Anne-Marie with him.

Meanwhile, the boys inside prison managed as well as any children wrongly convicted of a terrorist crime could be expected to. In some ways, they were like any other set of teenage brothers. Pat says Vince's five-year sentence 'all of a sudden turned into ten because I drove him mad, as you do with your big brother.' Once they were driven together to visit their mother in Durham's high security prison. 'We got into Durham at night, it's half 12, it's all locked up,' said Pat. 'We're walking along the landing and the screw's gone, "There you are, you're in there, and [Vince]'s gone," "Can I have a cell on my own?" and he thought he was joking. He said, "What's up with you? He's your brother!"'. Vince shot back, 'Yeah, I know; that's why I want a cell on my own'.[4]

Their mother recalled that when the two boys visited her, Pat, 'a boy in a man's prison, was wearing prison clothes which were way too big for him. He had to hold up his trousers with one hand the whole time to prevent them falling down.' While other prisoners put pictures of naked women up on the pin-board in their cell, Pat had photos of QPR football players on his.[5]

The two remained defiant, insisted on their innocence and found symbolic ways to protest. Pat, like his father, refused to close his own cell door at night. 'My dad said "Aren't they putting you away for long enough without you locking yourself up? You're doing their job for them," said Pat. He found other ways to remind the authorities they had wrongly jailed a child.

> On the card that used to be outside your door [they'd write] your name, your age, your sentence and they've got [a heading] 'Special Remarks' because you might need medicine or be a vegetarian or something. I wrote INNOCENT under that. When I came back they'd changed it and so I wrote it again and this went on for a few weeks. One day I came back and it's gone and there's a note saying come to the office. They took me to see the governor and he talked about destroying government property, the Home Office and all that. So I went back [to the card], took it out and I wrote it on the back – INNOCENT and stuck it back in. For the best part of my three years it was in there.

Few believed them and their story that they had nothing to do with the IRA, but slowly some minds began to change. Vince recalled:

> One particular screw, an SO [Senior Officer], was an ex-SAS man and for a year he gave me the evil eye. I was doing a catering course in the nick in Aylesbury and I asked for a job in the kitchens. It was a nice job because the little fiddles that were going on were things like you'd nick a lump of cheese for bartering – that's how innocent it was when we were there. He came to the cell in the night and I thought what does he want? He's never passed two words to me. He said, 'I believe you've applied for a position in the kitchens?' and I said, 'Yes, Mister Stone, I have,' and he said, 'I'm going to approve it but if you let me down I'll cut your bollocks off'. When I was in the kitchens Mister Stone said one day, 'You're not in the IRA, are you?' and I said, 'No, nothing to do with it.' He

> said, 'I know when someone's innocent or guilty and I know you're innocent but,' he said, 'life's a bollocks, innit.' He was the first one [in authority] who'd said that to me [that I was innocent].

Pat was released in March 1979. Nervous of coping in the outside world without his parents or older brother, he even asked if could be allowed to stay in prison until Vince was freed six months later. 'I've always said the sentence for me started when I got released,' said Pat. 'For other people coming out there was a mum or dad and I didn't have that.'

If they had been IRA members they would have been welcomed back into the bosom of republicanism. The campaigns to have the Guildford Four and Maguire convictions overturned had not really taken off when the boys were released, and they were left without any support. 'My sons were turfed out of the prison gates having served their sentences, to no social workers, no press or TV cameras' said Anne Maguire. 'They were still classed as convicted terrorists and had to get on with their lives as best they could, without the comfort of even having their parents or a family home.'[6] The boys were eventually put into a council flat together in a high-rise block without any carpet or furniture, but finding the basics was not the most difficult part of their release. Vince states:

> It was harder us being outside and my mum and dad inside. It was harder to come out to the real world where you had to earn a few bob and to go and visit your mum and dad. I was working in a hospital as a cook, getting paid peanuts. You'd have to go to the social security to get a pass to visit your mum and dad in prison. They'd say come in at nine o'clock and they'd make you wait til five o'clock. [Patrick] used to go there with a packed lunch and kip down all day – they'd give it to you so grudgingly.

Prison visits took on a new dynamic now the boys were free. It had somehow been easier to see their parents when they all knew they were going back to cells after the visit. After he was released, 'It was harder going to see them and leaving them,' said Vince.

> When we came out there was a campaign for the Guildford Four… we got brought into that – we were asked to participate and help in that. There's always been a bit of animosity between us and our cousin Gerry Conlon, and Paul Hill… But we thought it was for the common good – if people see they're innocent and we're innocent.

The animosity stemmed from before the arrests, when Conlon had stayed briefly with the Maguires in London. 'He was a silly young man who had caused his parents enough grief with his petty thieving,' said Anne Maguire, his aunt. 'Even when we took him in once to help him out for the sake of his parents, he stole from the children's piggy banks to feed his drug habit.'[7]

The struggle to have their names cleared publicly went on for many more frustrating years. After the convictions were publicly quashed in 1991. Vince and the rest of the Maguire family searched for an explanation for how they had come to be wrongly arrested and imprisoned in the first place.

> We all wanted to know why, why hasn't someone been brought to book about it? Someone, somewhere along the line did something either innocently, by mistake, or else tucked us up [framed us]… It's for the people who put us away to apologise. As time goes on they're dying off. I want [someone] to say to us, 'Look, you were tucked up,' or 'Look, it shouldn't have gone as far as it did. When you were in the Old Bailey we knew you weren't guilty. Up 'til then we thought you were but once all the evidence started coming through we thought it through a bit clearer, but we just went along with it because it kept everyone sweet, and we thought at the Court of Appeal you'd get out, that the appeal judges would look at it and say it's crap, let them out'.

John too is hoping that one day the police who helped convict his parents and brothers will tell their story. '… I'd love to see a couple of those coppers now, not for anything violent or anything but just to sit down and ask them – you must've had a beer after work or sat in the canteen and you must've talked to each other and said "I think there might be something wrong here",' he said.

The Maguires are still waiting for their explanation, and it might never come. Much about their case is still unresolved. They still do not know if they were deliberately framed to take pressure off a desperate police force, or whether they were victims of a series of innocent coincidental mistakes of forensic science. Whatever the truth behind their wrongful convictions, the strain of being innocent and constant campaigning to clear their names has been exhausting. 'I've often said over the years it might have been easier if we were guilty,' said Pat. 'If you'd done it, you'd go home and been a hero. The Balcombe blokes went back and were heroes. If we were guilty we wouldn't have to be going over the story for the last 20 years,' he said.

Much has happened to Vince since he wanted to be a policeman. His sense of Irish identity has been developed in extreme and unusual circumstances. He travelled the world for a year 'and people would say where are you from. I'd say London and they'd say it [Maguire]'s an Irish name and I'd say I'm geographically English and biologically Irish – that's the only way I can put it,' he said.

The Maguire, Guildford Four and Birmingham Six cases, plus thousands of cases of first and second generation Irish people detained under the PTA, resulted in a widespread fear in Irish communities that anyone could be framed and convicted for the most serious crimes. As the IRA continued to bomb England in the 1980s, Irish people and communities remained under constant suspicion.

South Londoner Jim Doherty began singing for a band – the Blue Eagles – as a teenager in the late 70s and early 80s. Like other members of the band, Doherty was second generation Irish, and the band played Irish dances and social clubs in London.

> We had been playing a mixture of Country and Western and Irish ballads for a number of years and the songs we did were pretty tame. We did a couple of rebel songs – *Sean South from Garryowen* and *James Connolly*. We played

> them first and foremost because they were good tunes. They always went down well at the Irish pubs and Irish clubs we played at and I can never recall anyone objecting, even though some of the lyrics were a bit 'strong'. For instance in *James Connolly* there is the line '...God's curse on you English, you cruel-hearted monsters, your deeds they would shame all the devils in hell.' I sometimes thought about the words I was singing as I am essentially English, but reconciled my thoughts as these songs were about events that happened back in 1916, no different to singing an English song that poured scorn upon the Germans but dated back to the First World War... [8]

The IRA bombed Harrod's on the afternoon of Saturday December 17, 1983. That night Doherty was due to play a gig at an Irish social club in London.

> For the first time ever we were approached by the manager who asked us to do no rebel songs and not to play the usual *Soldier's Song* at the end of the night. We substituted the national anthem with the hymn *Faith of Our Fathers* which became our standard goodnight call, from there on in, whenever we performed. And for a long time the verse that states '... with their tanks and their guns, oh my God what have they done?' was omitted from the song *The Town I Love So Well.*

Doherty clearly recalls the Harrod's bombing for other reasons too. 'I remember my father coming home the following week and telling us that some of his English colleagues at work has stopped speaking to him,' he said.

Conor Foley, a second generation Irish student, was arrested in 1985 a few weeks after a *World in Action* programme was aired which showed that the forensic tests which suggested that the Birmingham Six had been handling explosives might be flawed, and that the positive chemical results on their fingers could have been caused by the playing cards some of them had used shortly before they were arrested. When asked by police if 'you handle explosives during the course of your work?' he shot back, 'No, but I do have a set of playing cards.'[10]

The night after explosives were found outside Chelsea Barracks in London, Foley slept at a flat in Brixton on a friend's sofa.

> In the morning we were woken by armed police, when they broke down the front door with a sledge-hammer. We were dragged out of the flat, half-dressed, and put spread-eagled against a wall while they ripped the place apart with sledgehammers and crowbars. Police marksmen came down from the roof and, once outside, we saw that the whole street had been sealed off. We were taken to Paddington Green, a high-security police station, where we were held in solitary confinement for two days.

He was held incommunicado for most of that time and was questioned in the absence of a solicitor. Although held for less than the seven days permitted under the PTA, by the second day he was suffering from exhaustion and acute paranoia.

> I answered the police's questions as fully as I could, but I still felt ashamed when I gave them personal details such as the names and addresses of relatives in Ireland. I volunteered information because I wanted to get out of the situation as soon as possible. I knew that it was foolish to give a statement in the absence of a lawyer; it could only help to build the prosecution's case if I was charged. It is easy to see how people can make false confessions in such circumstances.

Although one of the custody officers (not an interrogating officer) said something about him being English, it was not a big issue, and he was not physically ill-treated or threatened at any point. Nor was there any verbal abuse. Foley doubted if the police ever really suspected him of being involved in a bomb plot. 'The questioning was very straightforward,' he said. 'Things like, "Where were you on the night of…? Can you prove it? When did you last go to Ireland? Where did you stay? What demonstrations have you been on?", etc. They questioned me about some things from my house, newspapers, etc.' They spent less than ten minutes questioning him about his movements on the night of the attempted bombing – the rest of the time they grilled him about his political views.

Despite his bravado in making the playing cards joke, Foley was genuinely scared about the swab tests on his hands.

> The forensic test that was conducted on my hands appeared to be the same as that performed on the Birmingham Six and Judy Ward. Knowing that these had given falsely positive results, I kept wondering what the police would do if mine also registered positive. Convictions were a foregone conclusion for anyone charged with an offence relating to Irish terrorism in the 1980s, and the usual sentence for those convicted was life imprisonment.

The arrest of Foley and his friend made front-page headlines in national newspapers, and the local Brixton paper, the *South London Press*, printed what Foley described as 'a completely fictitious claim which can only have been based on information from the police.' Under the heading: 'BOMB MAN HUNTED' the story reported that 'Anti-terrorist squad detectives are hunting a suspected Irish bomber who fled hours before a dawn swoop in South London this week. The man – wanted in connection with the bombs planted outside Chelsea Barracks – fled from a Brixton squat where two other men were detained on Wednesday. They were arrested as police stormed into their flat… but there was no trace of the third man.'[11]

Foley believed that by making arrests like his under the PTA the police could appear to the public as though they were making progress against terrorism, but were really just out to collect low-level political intelligence. 'I found out later that they had a very firm line of inquiry that took them in a completely different direction… so I don't really know why they bothered with us,' he said.

There are no figures available for how many of the thousands of people questioned under the Prevention of Terrorism Act were second generation, but in his study of the impact of the Act, released in 1993, Paddy Hillyard examined 115 individual cases of people detained, examined or arrested under the PTA in England, Scotland and Wales. Of those, he estimated that there were 'about 20 people that I knew were definitely second generation Irish. There could have been many more in the sample, but this information wasn't collected routinely.' Another study released in 1996 showed that until then about 6,500 people in England, Scotland and Wales had been arrested under the PTA, with many thousands more questioned and detained. Of those arrested under the PTA, 97 per cent were Irish. Yet despite all the arrests, only 3 per cent were finally charged. It is impossible to know how many second generation Irish people were caught up in the PTA, but the possibility of being questioned, detained, arrested and convicted for something you had not done was a constant threat to thousands of second generation Irish people in Britain during the Troubles.[12]

In December 1988 Clare Short, then Labour's frontbench spokesperson on employment, resigned in protest over the party's decision not to oppose the renewal of the *Prevention of Terrorism Act*. The Labour Party had opposed the bill's renewal before, but under increased pressure not to look soft on terrorism, the shadow cabinet had advised its MPs to abstain rather than vote against the PTA.

The Times reported that Short resigned before the vote took place 'with a sharply worded attack on Mr Kinnock's leadership. In a letter Ms Short said she was not willing to be "threatened or bullied… constant threats and denunciations simply reinforce the image of a divided and bickering party," she said. During the debate on the bill, Short said she could not support its renewal because, quite simply, 'the *Prevention of Terrorism Act* did not prevent terrorism.'[13]

10.
As Irish as the IRA

Tens of thousands of innocent Irish people were picked up under the PTA, and many more felt the cold stare of suspicion. While very few were active Republicans, and fewer still engaged in paramilitary activity, a core of second generation Republicans did emerge during the Troubles to play prominent and minor roles in paramilitary organisations. That a minority of second generation Irish people were prepared to go to war for the country they were not born in is not a uniquely Irish phenomenon.

In May 2003, 27 year-old Omar Khan Sharif, who was born and brought up in the British midlands, walked into a bar in Tel Aviv to blow himself up. Much of Britain was shocked that it could produce a suicide bomber. 'How could a second generation immigrant, a British citizen born and brought up [in Derby], turn his back on his cultural and religious roots and find in them a cause for which to both kill and to die?' asked one British newspaper.[1]

A substantial number of Republican paramilitaries, prepared to kill and die, were born and brought up in Britain. In early 1972 Reg Tester was a Command Staff Quartermaster for the Official IRA in Derry. Tester was from Nottinghamshire and had been in the British Navy.

He was by 1972 third in command of the local brigade. The city had an estimated 30 or 40 Official IRA members at the time. 'We relied heavily on propaganda to suggest that we were stronger than we actually were. For example, we did not have enough weapons to arm all 30 or 40 of our members,' he said.[2]

The Official IRA in Derry decided before Bloody Sunday to take what weapons they had out of the Bogside area of the city and into the Creggan district. As Quartermaster this was Tester's responsibility. 'The Official IRA was concerned that if everyone from the Creggan attended the march, leaving the Creggan empty, the Army would have invaded… All members of the Official IRA would have been in and out of headquarters in the Creggan during the 48 hours preceding the march and would have handed in their weapons then,' he said.

> After retrieving all weapons, they were kept in the boot of my car and another car… there were at least two people in my car and possibly two or three people in the other car… We had 30… weapons in the cars which ranged from rifles, submachine guns, handguns and boxes of ammunition. Both cars stayed at the centre of the Creggan that day. We drove around a bit and then stopped and parked for a while and then drove around a bit again. At some time that afternoon we had stopped on the New Road and word reached us that something had happened in the Bogside. My orders had been not to do anything. However, I was only human and wanted to hit back at the Army. After what had happened, some people had a go at us and said "What are you doing here, you should be down in the Bogside".

Active in that early period too was Joe Gilhooley. Gilhooley – known as 'English Joe' because he was from Manchester – moved to Dublin in 1970. He was jailed for IRA membership in 1975 and spent eight months in Portlaoise prison. British police also wanted to question him about a series of attacks in England the year before, including explosions at Aldershot and Warminster and a bomb at Edward Heath's home. He was rearrested at the gates of Portlaoise prison as walked he out, the subject of an extradition order by Scotland Yard. Gilhooley successfully evaded extradition after he appealed to the High Court in Dublin that his offences were political.[3]

Liam Heffernan became involved in Republicanism through left-wing English politics. Also from Lancashire, he had been born and brought up in Manchester of Irish parents, and was found guilty in December 1993 of conspiracy to steal explosives and to cause explosions, as well as firearms offences. He was reported to be a member of the Irish National Liberation Army (INLA) and was sentenced to 23 years in prison.

Pat Hayes and Jan Taylor were convicted of IRA activity in 1994, including bombing Harrod's, and each sentenced to 30 years in prison. Hayes was third generation Irish, Taylor English. The police were astonished that such men would join the IRA. 'There was a gap in our intelligence,' said one police source. 'It is almost without precedent for two born-and-bred Englishmen to be terrorists at this level. By any objective analysis these people would not be considered as IRA suspects.'[4]

Hayes had a degree in business studies and had worked in the late 1980s for Sainsbury's as a programmer and analyst. Taylor was a former soldier in the British Army who had served in Cyprus and had been awarded a UN peace medal. He left the British Army in 1973, and later worked for British Telecom. Like Heffernan, they entered the world of Irish Republican paramilitaries through revolutionary ideology.

There is no one simple explanation for why second generation Irish people chose to join the IRA. For some it was a predominantly socialist motivation, for others it may have been an effort to establish a 'super-Irish' identity, and for others still because of a highly developed sense of ideological Republicanism. Unsurprisingly, the motivation seems to have been rooted in a series of factors rather than one specific belief or incident.

According to Seán MacStiofáin, 'Three groups of people join the IRA: One, in the north – growing up watching the RUC and all that – they were pushed into the IRA. Then, in both the north and south, those who join from family tradition. The third category is those who've decided the best way to obtain the unity and freedom of all Ireland is to join the movement... These people, the third group, are more... you get good people from the other groups but people who've studied it and say the only way is armed struggle through the revolutionary movement are best. Those with no tradition or connection with the movement are a minority.'[5]

In December 1998, as part of the Peace Process, a small group of Republican prisoners was flown to Irish prisons from English jails. Among them was Michael Gallagher, born and brought up in Glasgow. 'There were four of us going to Portlaoise on the plane,' he said. 'All four of us were born outside Ireland – me, Jimmy Murphy, Jan Taylor and Paddy Kelly and here we were in the air, getting repatriated to Ireland...'[6]

Gallagher grew up in Scotland of Irish parents. As a child, he went to Donegal on holidays and remembered 'visiting the GPO for the first time as a child and it did impress me, things like that,' he said.

As a schoolboy in the 1950s, 'I would've classed myself as Irish because of my father and mother,' he said. 'I went to the Gaelic League in Glasgow and learned Irish Gaelic when I was six years of age. In the house I used to hear Irish regularly. Although my mother and father didn't speak it between themselves there would be social events in my house, like cards and the people who came up – mostly men – would be speaking Irish. We could have two conversations in my house at the one time – a group of people speaking Irish and the children and my mother and her friends speaking English,' he said.

'The school I went to – I don't think the Irishness really kicked in there until the Troubles started. There was a certain tendency in my school to offload the Irishness. Maybe 70-80 per cent were from an Irish background, but there was definitely a move at that time to get rid of the Irishness and to be Jock and Scots and all this carryon,' he said. Gallagher's early identification as Irish expressed itself through an anti-Scotishness.

'We supported England against Scotland, would you believe. You'd find most people [of Irish descent] would be anti-English, right, but we actually supported England against Scotland… when I was a kid we supported England. I remember a game here, Scotland playing Costa Rica, and we were so pleased that Costa Rica beat Scotland… they were just so sectarian, so much of the north [of Ireland] all over again,' he recalled.

'I was about 18 when I got a passport. I'll tell you something – I had no problems, I just got a British passport. I didn't even think of it. There was never even a debate. I didn't get an Irish passport til maybe 12 years ago. I'll tell you something else I used to do… I used to swear an oath to the Queen, and I was in the cubs and you had to dib dib, swear your oath to the king or whatever. I used to do that routinely…'.

But he also remembered 'a fascination about [the North]. When things flared up in the north it was just great, it was terrific. I mean we always came through the north to Donegal and I used to stay for a week most years in Claudy, outside Derry, and my uncles were in the lowly paid jobs and they didn't have a vote… and when the flareup came it was wonderful,' he said.

In 1998, Gallagher was convicted at Woolwich Crown Court, south-east London, of conspiracy to cause explosions. He was found guilty of helping with mortar attacks on Heathrow Airport. The mortars were fired at the airport on three days in March 1994, and failed to explode. In sentencing him to 20 years in prison, Justice Tucker told Gallagher: 'You played a vital role in a highly organised and determined bombing attack on Heathrow Airport. This series of attacks resulted in enormous disruption of services and it was in my view purely fortuitous that there was no injury or loss of life or extensive damage.'[7]

Gallagher had been the target of a staggering surveillance operation. His conversations were secretly recorded over two and a half years by Special Branch and MI5 until his arrest in 1996. He was followed around London and on visits to Northern Ireland and to Dublin. Gallagher was once followed by 29 police officers across London who suspected he was about to meet a senior IRA figure. But Gallagher and the other man walked past each other, without any obvious hint of recognition, when Gallagher apparently suspected he was being watched.

After the bombing of London's Canary Wharf in February 1996 that ended a 17-month IRA ceasefire, Republican sympathisers in London came under increased scrutiny from the police. Patrick Kelly, one of the prisoners on the plane with Gallagher going to Portlaoise at the end of 1998, and others became targets of the biggest ever surveillance operation mounted by the Metropolitan Police.

Kelly was born in Birmingham in 1966 but moved to Longford a few years later. 'Being born in England was par for the course where I came from', he said. Because of emigration to and from England's midlands in the late 1950s, Kelly 'was one of seven or eight out of a class of 20 who had been born in England,' he said.[8]

'I always considered in my teen years that people didn't have to be from Ireland to be a Republican. I was aware of British presence in the six counties but I didn't see it in Longford. I based my Republicanism on the 1798 variety – I didn't see that people had to be Catholic or born in Ireland to be Republican. I knew at school that Ireland had a long tradition of Republicans born outside of Ireland. That they were Republican-minded was the main thing,' he recalled.

'The [1980/81] hunger strikes would've been the first time that I attended my first demonstration – in Longford. It was quite a big demonstration for somewhere like Longford, the second smallest county in Ireland. I also wore a black armband at school that was frowned on because people here had their head in the sands, ostrich-like since 1923,' he said.

'We were at Mass once and the priest asked the congregation to pray for a British soldier that had been killed and my father shouted up [from the pew] "What about the hungerstrikers!" – three or four hunger strikers had died at this time – "You never asked us to pray for them!" Now at my age I admire him for it but at the time you'd die from the cringe factor,' he said.

Kelly was arrested in September 1996 in a police raid on a hotel room in west London. Kelly was convicted of conspiracy to cause explosions and possessing explosives with intent. He was sentenced to 20 years in prison. With Kelly in the hotel room was Diarmuid O'Neill, who was shot dead by the police during the raid.

Diarmuid O'Neill was born at Queen Charlotte's Hospital in Hammersmith, west London on June 24 1969 with impressive Republican credentials. His grandfather was Domhnall O'Buachalla from Maynooth in Kildare, who had led a contingent of Irish Volunteers from the town to Dublin to join the Easter Rising in 1916. He had been interned at Frongoch internment camp in Wales with hundreds of other Volunteers. O'Buachalla was elected to prisoners' governing body in the camp, the camp's general council (or 'General Council or Civil Government of the Irish Republic in Frongoch' as it ambitiously described itself.)[9]

He was released in the general amnesty of Christmas 1916, and was duly elected as a TD to the first Dáil in the 1918 elections, representing Kildare. He sided with the anti-Treaty IRA in the civil war, and was close to de Valera. A founder member of Fianna Fáil, O'Buachalla was appointed Governor-General by de Valera in 1932 in a deliberate attempt to undermine the office. A vestige of the 1921 Treaty, the Governor-General position remained as testament that Ireland was still, officially, a British dominion. O'Buachalla agreed to do the minimum necessary, and signed pieces of paper when they needed to be signed. He didn't move into the Vice Regal Lodge, was paid £2,000 a year instead of the £28,000 given to his predecessor, and never appeared formally at any public occasion. The office, and all that it stood for, sunk without trace. O Buachalla died six years before Diarmuid O'Neill was born, but his career has not been forgotten – several of the artefacts he made in Frongoch are on display in the National Museum of Ireland.

O'Neill's childhood was spent in a typically second generation Irish fashion – holidays in Ireland, education at a local Catholic school in England. O'Neill's younger brother Shane recalled: 'We had a cottage up in Donegal, right beside the sea. A 200 year-old cottage and us coming over from London to the extremes and now we're in a three-roomed cottage by the sea at the foot of a mountain. It was just beautiful, and we just had fun all the time.'[10]

Their parents, Eoghan and Theresa O'Neill, had settled in Hammersmith in the 1960s and brought up their three children in London before retiring to west Cork in the early '90s. Diarmuid and Shane went to the London Oratory school, a Catholic secondary school in London with a reputation for turning out well-spoken students with academic qualifications. British Prime Minister Tony Blair sent his son Euan to be educated there.

Headmaster John McIntosh said Diarmuid 'and his brother, Shane… were very pleasant and courteous boys who got on with their work… [Diarmuid was] a boy with bright ginger hair. He was a well-behaved boy who got on well with anybody. He just got on with his work here. He went through school keeping his head down. He was just a very pleasant boy who was never in trouble.' Paddy Kelly, who knew O'Neill well in London, said 'Diarmuid had a slightly upmarket accent… He used to put it on a bit, the London twang, for street cred'.[11]

At weekends, from the age of about 15, O'Neill went on Republican marches and rallies, and sold the Republican newspaper *An Phoblacht* in Irish pubs and community centres in west London. O'Neill left school at 17, and was soon in considerable trouble. In 1988 he started work as a junior clerk at the Shepherd's Bush branch of the Bank of Ireland, but within a year was found guilty of embezzling £75,000. Half of it wound up in a newly opened bank account in Belfast, believed to be connected to the Republican movement. A draft for the rest of the money was also taken, but never cashed. Forced to leave his job, O'Neill was convicted on five fraud charges and sent to jail in June 1989. As he had already served two months on remand, he was freed after five further months in custody at Finnamore Wood young offenders' institution in Berkshire.[12]

British press reports suggest that as soon as O'Neill was released he visited the IRA contact in west Cork who had recruited him in 1988. O'Neill was a regular visitor to the area. The Irish Republican press suggested that 'When he joined the IRA, he volunteered to work in the area he knew best – England – knowing that it was the most dangerous place in the world for an Irish Republican.'[13]

Kelly dismissed the suggestion that O'Neill was naïve and led astray by a member of the Cork IRA. 'Diarmuid got his republicanism through a deep interest in politics. He wasn't one of these people who had to do something to prove he was more Irish than anybody else,' he said. 'He felt duty bound for himself to do something about it. His motivation wasn't because he went home [to Ireland] on holidays and met a shady guy in a pub who fooled him into it – he was one of those young, bright, articulate intelligent people who once they found out some home truths about [the situation] could do like everyone else and avoid it and live with the discomfort of doing nothing, or could do something about it. He was very much a person who practised what he preached.'

Kelly lived in London from 1987 to 1992. 'Myself and Diarmuid O'Neill spent a lot of time together in England and had many conversations about Republicanism. I asked Diarmuid about his attitude to the thinking of Irish-born people or English-born people in London. Diarmuid was shot on the Monday morning and I remember asking him about this in a conversation on the Saturday, just a couple of days before. His background and his accent were very much London and it didn't identify him as Irish,' he said.

Kelly asked O'Neill if his second generation identity raised any issues when he talked about the Troubles with Irish-born people. 'It annoyed him especially when he went to Ireland, or in conversations with Irish-born people living in England… when a conversation would be initiated about the six counties and the conflict. It used to animate him somewhat when people would make a disparaging comment like – he was highly politicised and highly articulate – and people would invariably say to him "how would you know anything about it? You're from England",' said Kelly.

'And it used to really annoy him. He said to me: "If you extended their logic to the understanding of the conflict, why would Ian Paisley have a different opinion from Gerry Adams or John Hume if being from there was a prerequisite to understanding the conflict?" Obviously you have a conflict and people who live there in houses next to each other have totally opposing views so he was very aware of that, and he said to me that people always threw that into the mix, into the conversation, that somehow because you weren't from there you couldn't know anything about it. He was surprised that I said people say it to me because I was from Longford,' said Kelly.

The month before Kelly was arrested, he was spotted on a security camera at a London tube station with Brian McHugh from Fermanagh. They were then seen with Diarmuid O'Neill and Jimmy Murphy, a friend of O'Neill's who was a schools' groundsman.

Murphy was born in London to Irish parents, and grew up in Fulham with regular holidays to Limerick and Dublin. His was not a particularly Republican family but he read about Irish history from the age of about twelve or thirteen, and became aware of the part played by British-born figures 'like James Connolly and Tom Clarke' in the 1916 Rising. This was around the time of the hungers strikes of 1981 and like many others, he cited them as a key formative experience.[14]

Although he was called Plastic Paddy 'on an odd occasion,' he said it was relatively easy to identify himself as Irish in London. While Murphy regarded himself as Irish and supported Ireland – not England – at football, he was content to have a British passport. 'My first passport was when I was about 20… I had a British passport. I needed a passport quickly. There was a problem with getting a certificate for the Irish passport so I got the British one. It wasn't a big deal,' he said.

A few years later, Murphy was in deep trouble as the watching security services realised he was involved with an Active Service Unit of the IRA. McHugh was the leader of the unit. O'Neill was the quartermaster and for some time he'd been amassing weapons and explosives.

O'Neill used the alias of Ray Wilkinson and posed as a haulage contractor. He rented a lockup garage in Hornsey in north London in which was stored six tonnes of homemade explosives, two pounds of semtex, power units, detonators, three AK47s and two handguns. A huge team of police and MI5 officers followed the unit in a plan codenamed Operation Tinnitus. Kelly booked into a Butlin's holiday camp in north Wales under an assumed name and then went to south Yorkshire to collect a Ford Cargo lorry. The police followed him there and back. The surveillance operation involved 250 officers.

Listening bugs were placed in O'Neill's car. The tapes of the conversation, obtained by the excellent BBC TV *Spotlight* programme, show how the police heard O'Neill tell Kelly how he prepared to plant a bomb. 'The way it's being done now I'm gonna wire it. I have done a few engineering camps,' he said.

They also heard O'Neill tell Kelly what he would do if the police came to arrest him. 'Well I would imagine if it's going to happen the way they'll do it is they've got the place rigged already – they'll have a couple of lorries with boys on them. We'll be working away and next thing fucking bright lights all around and it will just be "This is the police, you're surrounded – come out with your hands up." If that's the case I'm coming out with my fucking hands up… I'm coming out. You could be in out in five years for fuck's sake,' said O'Neill.[15]

The police decided to raid the hotel room where O'Neill, Kelly and McHugh were staying. SO19, the Metropolitan Police's elite firearms unit, was briefed at its Old Street headquarters before the raid and shown videos of the Canary Wharf explosion. They also decided to use rip gas, a kind of CS gas never used in London before. The security services twice entered and filmed the room when the IRA men were out. They found no arms.

A few minutes after 4.30 in the morning police vehicles and an ambulance were parked close to the hotel and armed officers moved in and took up positions outside Room 303. The police tried to open the door with a key card but it didn't work. A battering ram was used to try and break the door but it bounced off. By now the men in the room had woken up. Kelly took refuge in the bathroom.

Five ripgas pellets were fired in through the bedroom window while another five gas cartridges were fired into the room from inside. O'Neill was closest to the door and shouted 'We give up – whoa. We're unarmed.'[16]

A police taperecording of the raid that night shows O'Neill trying to surrender.

> Police: 'I am a police officer. Get on the floor… Come to the fucking door now.
>
> O'Neill: 'Ok. We're down.'
>
> Police: 'Show me your hands now.'
>
> O'Neill: 'They're up, they're up. We're on the deck.'
>
> Police: 'Show me your hands through the door, show me your hands through the door… Shoot the fuckers.'

The policeman who shot Diarmuid O'Neill has only been identified by his codename of Officer Kilo. 'Through the smoke of the gas I could see a figure standing at the door,' said Kilo. 'He said nothing. His bodylanguage appeared aggressive because his upper body was leaning towards me. I had nowhere to go so I moved towards him, firing two shots. I felt as if nothing had happened because the figure was in exactly the same position. He had not moved. I thought I had missed, so I fired a further two pairs of shots from my MP5. My torchbeam was on, but it was being dissipated by gas. I pushed the figure backwards into the room,' he said in a statement. Kilo was one of several police officers who left his respirator behind, and whose vision was impaired when the CS gas was released.[17]

Brian McHugh said O'Neill was surrendering when shot. In a statement to the BBC he said 'I was in a crouched position beside the bed I'd been sleeping in and almost directly to Diarmuid's left, and slightly behind him. Diarmuid was trying to answer both policemen, saying "okay, okay" to the man asking him to open the door and "we're on the deck" to the second policeman. One of them shouted "open this fucking door now. Open this fucking door now" was repeated again. In answer to one of the men Diarmuid said he couldn't open the door, that it wouldn't open. One of them said "open it, open it". The policeman fired two shots, hitting Diarmuid. Diarmuid said "Fucking hell," surprised that shooting had started now access had been given to the room.'[18]

O'Neill, like both the other men in the room, was unarmed. He was shot six times. Three policemen carried him outside. Surveillance footage shows that as he was carried out his head bounced off one of the steps. He was bleeding heavily, but still alive. No explosives or weapons were found in the room. O'Neill was put on the pavement and given first aid, and 20 minutes later placed in an ambulance and taken to Charing Cross Hospital, where he died.

Shane O'Neill insists his brother was surrendering when he was killed. 'You could hear it on the tape – "We give up, We're unarmed. We're on the deck. We give up". He was complying with whatever the police asked him to do he was doing it. He got to the door, he tried to open it, and they shot him six times,' he said.[19]

Diarmuid O'Neill had been closely monitored in the days before the raid. The police filmed him up a ladder painting the outside of his parents' house. Tina Cuenco, who ran a newsagents near O'Neill's parents' home saw him a few hours before he was killed. "Diarmuid was always buying chocolate from us. He couldn't get enough. That night he was very unshaven and looked all done in. I assumed that he had been working too hard – I knew he had been decorating." The police were watching him so closely they even recorded what chocolate bars he bought that night.[20]

O'Neill's family still don't know why he wasn't arrested at a time when it would have been so easy for the police to apprehend him – on the way to the shop the night before he died, or halfway up the ladder. O'Neill's girlfriend Karmele Erono was surprised to discover his IRA involvement. 'I was shocked – you find out someone you lived with and was very close to you [was in the IRA] and you haven't known anything, you haven't noticed anything ... Diarmuid was a Republican, definitely a Republican. He could not understand people in Ireland being treated the way they were being treated for the sake of being Irish. He couldn't comprehend that and he used to get upset about and give out about it. He felt for them, even though he wasn't born there. He did feel for them,' she said.[21]

Oliver Donohue, a family friend of the O'Neill's in London, said: 'I was quite amazed how Irish he was because his parents were definitely not over-emphatic about their Irish origins. They just participated in normal community activities and their children similarly. Their sister Siobhan became a nurse and a sister in the local [Kensington and Chelsea] hospital. They grew up as a normal family. It was a great surprise to all of us that he was so involved,' he said.[22]

In February 2000 a coroner's jury in south London found O'Neill's death was one of lawful killing, and no charges were brought against any police officers. Some of O'Neill's family and friends have pushed for a public inquiry into his death. In December 1997 the others were sentenced. Brian McHugh got 25 years for conspiring to cause explosions, Kelly 20 years and James Murphy seventeen years.

One of Murphy's fellow inmates in prison, a bank robber, 'went on one of these courses to accept your crime – it was basically an agenda to get people out of jail – that's why they went on these courses,' recalled Murphy. 'He told me one of the screws had said to him "We have lots of different people on this wing – we have Traitor Scum," which he said meant me.'

Of his old London schoolmates today, Murphy said some of them 'might be bitter towards me' for what he did. 'But a lot of them I knew personally, and would say [I] did my own thing.'

The police raid on the hotel and the killing of Diarmuid O'Neill contrasted sharply with the successful and non-violent end to the siege at Balcombe Street 21 years earlier. Four IRA men – Harry

Duggan, Hugh Doherty, Joe O'Connell, and Eddie Butler – were cornered by police in London's west end after a car chase. The four broke into a council flat in Balcombe Street and took a couple in their 50s as hostages. The police laid siege to the flat for six days before the men finally gave themselves up and released the two hostages unharmed. Hugh Doherty was from Glasgow. He had been born and brought up in the city and joined the IRA.

Doherty, a former altar-boy, left school at 15. He worked on building sites in London and Dublin and in late 1974 joined the IRA unit in London, after other members of the unit had carried out the Guildford pub bombings. By December 11 he was operating with the team, and that night he and Joe O'Connell bombed the Naval and Military club in Mayfair before escaping in a car. On August 27 the following year Doherty and Duggan planted a bomb in a soldiers' pub in Caterham in Surrey. The pub was popular with the Welsh Guards, who had just returned to barracks nearby after a tour of duty in Northern Ireland. No-one was killed in the attack, but 33 people were injured.[23]

The four men were among the most prolific IRA operators of the Troubles. *The Daily Telegraph* described them as 'the best team the Provos ever had'. They began attacking targets in and around London in the autumn of 1974 and in the year before they were captured they averaged about one attack every week. Ross McWhirter, a right-wing activist and TV personality, was shot dead on his doorstep after offering a reward for the unit's capture.

Another member of the prolific IRA team in London – though not one of those caught at Balcombe Street – was second generation Irishman Liam Quinn from San Francisco. Quinn's father was Irish and his mother Mexican. Quinn grew up in the turbulent radical atmosphere of the Bay area in the late 1960s, but instead of protesting against the Vietnam War, like many of his contemporaries, Quinn became involved in Irish Republicanism. In 1971 he was in his early twenties and was working for the US Mail service, but quit to go to Ireland and join the Republican movement. 'I saw it as the struggle that had lasted for 100 years before being resumed again,' he said.[24]

According to local San Francisco sources, Quinn was introduced to the IRA by Chuck Malone, a Republican active in Irish America for several decades who was known in the US media as the 'Golden Gate Gunrunner' after being charged with smuggling arms to the IRA in the 1970s. Quinn was reportedly recruited into the IRA by Malone, who personally escorted him to Derry in September 1971 where introductions were made.[25] Quinn, a US citizen, was eventually convicted of murdering PC Stephen Tibbett, a 21 year-old unarmed police officer who was shot dead after confronting Quinn in London in February 1975. After the killing Quinn fled London and was arrested later the same year in Dublin and sentenced to 12 months' imprisonment for IRA membership. Quinn returned to San Francisco on his release from prison in Ireland, but was rearrested in California in 1981 by the FBI and in 1986 lost a protracted legal battle against extradition to the UK. Quinn claimed unsuccessfully that his actions in England for the IRA were political, and so he ought not to be extradited. He was returned to England and in 1988 was sentenced to life imprisonment for murdering PC Tibbett.

'I wanted to help out if I could. I'd do it all over again. I'm afraid I would,' he said. 'I guess that nice American boy wasn't happy with the television culture and the Disneyland world. I guess he was looking for a new identity and better sense of values and just happened to find a worthy cause to be devoted to'. Ten years later Quinn was transferred to Portlaoise Prison in Ireland before being released as part of the Peace Process in April 1999. He had been, with Doherty, a key IRA Volunteer in London in the early 1970s.[26]

Doherty stole the cars used on several operations, and used a series of aliases in London, including John Anderson and Don Kelly. By December 1975 he was sharing a flat in north London with Eddie Butler where they slept in sleeping bags on top of bare mattresses. The first Saturday afternoon of that month Doherty stole a dark blue Ford Cortina to use in the evening's planned operation – a return to a previous target, Scott's Bar in Mayfair.

With Duggan, O'Connell and Butler, Doherty drove to the west end that night and as the car passed Scott's, O'Connell leaned out of the window and fired into the restaurant. Police spotted the incident and gave chase, cornering them in Balcombe St.[27]

In 1977, aged 26, Doherty stood trial at the Old Bailey with the others. He refused to recognise the court. He was given eleven life sentences, one term of 21 years, five terms of twenty years, and one of eighteen years. He responded by shouting 'Good luck, Mary' to his sister in the public gallery.[28]

In early 1998, Doherty and the others had been transferred from prison in England to Portlaoise as part of the Peace Process, and on Sunday May 10 they were allowed out on day release to attend the Sinn Féin Ard Fheis in Dublin. The men were given a ten-minute cheering, shouting ovation and described by Gerry Adams as 'our Nelson Mandelas'.[29]

11.
Identity Politics

While Hugh Doherty was serving his prison sentence, his brother Pat rose to become a senior Republican. He is currently Sinn Féin MP for West Tyrone and Vice President of Sinn Féin, although he too was born and brought up in Glasgow.

'What made Glasgow very different from any other British city was the huge number of people from Donegal, and particularly the Gaeltacht area,' said Pat Doherty. 'It would not have been unusual in the Gorbals areas where I was born and grew up to hear Irish spoken on the street. My parents spoke it. I'd have seen kids growing up whose parents were from Gaeltacht area speaking Irish with a Glasgow accent.'[1]

Growing up, the Doherty boys spent every spare minute they could in Ireland. 'I went to Ireland every summer holidays and any opportunity in between for as long as I could remember,' said Pat. 'We used to call it the Derry boat – the boat left Glasgow at five o'clock in the evening and got into Derry about seven the next morning. That was the traditional route. I think I remember counting one time I was on it 28 times and there was a similar boat that went to Belfast and I was on that ten times.'

Pat Doherty left home at the age of thirteen to become a priest. He spent four and a half years studying as a seminarian before he left. 'I remember when I was at college [seminary] we were all brought to see Ben Hur at the cinema in Scotland and they played God Save the Queen. At least half the class sat in their seats and I don't think God Almighty would've made me stand up,' he recalled.

'I also remember while at college reading My Fight For Irish Freedom [by IRA civil war leader Dan Breen]-I can't even remember how I got the book. Those books weren't in my home,' he said. 'I remember having it under the desk and reading it during lessons. Really that was that – I left college and I really wasn't at all interested [in politics]. I had this growing thing that I was Irish, and if I was Irish why was I living in Scotland? Why not go and live in Ireland?'

Doherty married in 1967 and moved to Ireland early the following year, aged 23. He got a job in Derry in construction as a site engineer against overwhelming odds as emigration was all in the opposite direction at the time. 'At this stage I wasn't really political, but certainly feeling very Irish,' he said. 'I would've been a million times more acutely aware of my accent then than I am now.'

Doherty said he was influenced by a series of political realisations in those first years in Ireland. 'The most defining one was one day the director asked me to pay out the wages because he wanted to go off early and I was really shocked by the wages – I just didn't know. These were married men with families and they were getting less than what I would have got as a bonus back in Glasgow. It really hit me between the eyes. So I started to read – I started to read ferociously. The civil rights movement was just starting. I wasn't involved but I was observing everything that was happening and was reading, reading,' he said.

In August 1969 he was in Derry. 'The Yanks around the same time [at the end of July] landed a man on the moon and I remember standing at the top of William St in Derry when the British soldiers had arrived in Derry in August '69. I remember saying to myself for fuck's sake what's happening here? The

Yanks have landed somebody on the moon and I am seeing British soldiers landing in Ireland again.'

Doherty joined Sinn Féin in April 1970, despite a certain self-consciousness about his accent. 'In early Sinn Féin meetings I'd be wary [of speaking] – they'll think I'm a Brit or something,' he recalled. But at British Army checkpoints 'my accent was of immense use because they took the wrong assumption and I didn't, as they say in Donegal, "put them past their notion"'.

On Bloody Sunday Doherty was at home in Donegal. A relative from Derry was visiting and when the news of the unarmed protestors being shot by the British Army began to filter in he immediately left to drive her to Derry. 'I remember being there on the day of the funeral and there were a lot of politicians from the south there and I remember having absolute disdain for them and thinking to myself that's the only time they've been across the border,' he recalled.

Some political analysts claim Doherty became an important IRA figure. Veteran political journalist and author Ed Moloney claimed in a 2002 book that Doherty was on the IRA's Army Council in the 1980s and 1990s. Similar charges are routinely levelled at virtually all prominent Sinn Féin figures, and is one which – predictably – Doherty denies.[2]

Doherty is one of several current Republican political activists from the diaspora. Kieran Clifford was born in Brooklyn in1965, and is third generation Irish. As a child growing up in New York, she recalled her family regularly attended an Easter Mass to commemorate of the 1916 Rising, and the hunger strikes of the early 1980s also made an impact on her.

She moved to Dublin in 2000 after having worked in the Friends of Sinn Féin office in Washington DC in the late 1990s. She knew from her experience with Irish Republicans in the US that in Ireland she 'would be viewed as a blow-in,' and 'as yet another mad Yank who had romanticised notions of the struggle'.[3]

Undeterred, Clifford threw herself into Sinn Féin activity, joining the local cumann in Dublin. She became the party's

Director of Canvass during the first *No to Nice* referendum, and was Director of Elections for the local candidate's campaign in the 2002 general election.

She also worked fulltime for the Sinn Féin newspaper *An Phoblacht /Republican News* for 16 months, before becoming Programme Director of Tar Isteach, a community development project aimed at Republican ex-prisoners.

She suggested her background meant she could offer a different perspective on issues. 'I think I am less likely to fall into Irish patterns of behaviour that can be somewhat destructive... I don't buy into the begrudgery thing and also I am always willing to try new things in terms of raising awareness and pushing the issues. Another thing is that I am not automatically suspicious and critical of new people,' she said.

She sometimes finds her New York upbringing liberating. 'I don't have to adhere to all the crap about knowing your place and doing things the way they have always been done because I am different right from the start,' she said.

Despite her impressive Republican credentials, Clifford has no illusions about how she is viewed. 'I don't even try to claim an Irish identity. Locals don't accept I am Irish. They never will. How could you even suppose they would when they refer to other Irish people who have only been three generations in their neighbourhood as blow-ins? I just take it for granted that I will always be considered an outsider' she said.

Theresa Moriarty is also active in Sinn Féin. She was born in London to Irish parents and her west Kerry father ran a pub in Camberwell, south London, during the 1950s. Neither of her parents were Republicans. 'There wasn't much in the way of rebel songs in our house,' she said. 'My mother [from Kilkenny] even used to say that the Black and Tans weren't all bad. She gave the anecdote of the time that the Tans had gone into their house, a small little thatched cottage with God knows how many kids. The Tans had turned up to loot the house for food, and there wasn't any in the house, so they went away. So they went away to rob the big farm up the road and they brought back food to the kids.'[4]

As a teenager Moriarty started to listen to Irish music and reading Irish history books, but was frustrated by the few opportunities in London to develop an Irish political interest. 'I did once attempt to join Cumann na mBan [Republican women's wing],' she said, 'but I couldn't find out how to do it. I was about seventeen or eighteen and I saw someone with a badge on a tube and she was gone before I could speak to her.'

In the 1980s she moved from London to the home in west Kerry where her father had grown up, but it wasn't until she made her first visit to the north of Ireland in the early 1990s that she became a Republican. 'Going to the north wiped the scales from my eyes,' she said. 'I was in a small street – Mary Street – in Warrenpoint, and I looked out the window and there were six soldiers marching with their rifles out and I was overwhelmed with outrage. It was a bit of anger with myself that I'd ignored this all these years… I had the history and the knowledge, but it's so important to be there to see it,' she said.

'When I went to Belfast I just couldn't believe it…I didn't know the barricade along the Falls Road was the way it was. It was just so permanent, and so appalling to look at… and then tanks with soldiers sticking out the top. It was overwhelming,' she said. 'I went over the border a Nationalist, and I came back a tearing Republican.' Shortly after returning to her home in west Kerry, and more than 90 years after Londoner Desmond Fitzgerald set up the Irish Volunteers on the Dingle peninsula, it was Theresa Moriarty who founded a Sinn Féin cumman in the same area.

Throughout the course of the Troubles, and of the earlier conflicts, many second generation Irish people from London and elsewhere played key roles in the development of Irish Republicanism. Other second generation figures, often wearing British Army uniforms, fought against them.

12.
Misfit Soldiers

Edward Casey was born in London's east end of Irish parents in 1898. As a teenager he signed up with the Royal Dublin Fusiliers because of his Irish heritage, but immediately noticed tension in the regiment between English- and Irish-born soldiers. Casey appeared to be the only English-born soldier in the company sent for training to Cork, and was picked on by his colleagues. He was only accepted by the rest of the soldiers when he told them he had relatives in Limerick, after which he was subjected to an initiation ceremony which involved him being thrown around in a blanket.[1]

Conscription because of the First World War soon diluted the Fusiliers from its heavily Irish base, and Casey identified himself as 'Cockney Irish' to set himself apart from the new English influx. Casey proved no model soldier, and had a chequered career in the British Army which included several spells fighting in Europe, deserting while in France, successfully faking shellshock to be sent away from the trenches, going absent without leave in Dublin, deserting while in London and – unsurprisingly – a few spells in military prison.

Casey's account of his military career, *The Misfit Soldier*, recounts how he was sent to Ireland before the Easter Rising, where his experience was full of contradictions over his identity.

He started seeing an Irish girl in Cork who was attacked by Sinn Féin and had her head shaved for consorting with the enemy. She was finally forced to leave the country and live in Liverpool because of her association with Casey.

When Casey decided to visit his relatives in Limerick, he discovered they were republicans and one was an active Volunteer. After an initially chilly welcome into the family home, his Volunteer cousin took Casey to the pub, where the locals were astonished to see the British soldier. The cousin introduced him to the crowd by quoting Jesus: 'We forgive you, you know not what you do' to general amusement, and Casey was given a friendly welcome. But when his cousin tried to tell Casey he was really Irish – 'You're a full-blooded Irishman, born in the wrong place' – Casey reacted strongly and confusedly, and insisted he was a Cockney, 'from the biggest city in the whole bleeding world'.[2]

Casey's account tells how he was sent to help put down the Easter Rising, and discovered that many of his British Army colleagues were Liverpool-Irish. He was stationed at the Four Courts during the Easter Rising, and witnessed the surrender of several key Volunteers, including Markievicz, 'a foreigner called De Valera' and many others.[3]

He then went absent without leave while in Dublin, was arrested and confined to barracks. There, confusingly, he found British soldiers who said they supported Sinn Féin. Casey was eventually sent back to London, where he promptly deserted, was rearrested and volunteered to go to Bulgaria to fight rather than go to prison. Then he successfully feigned memory loss and was sent to a military hospital in Malta.

In the early years of the recent conflict, some British soldiers with Irish ancestry or Catholic upbringings, or both, felt similar confusion to Casey about their role. Jimmy Johnson of the Royal Tank Regiment was sent to Lurgan in 1972 for a four-month tour of duty. One Sunday, with other soldiers, he was searching a house in a small housing estate in Portadown.

> I said to Lieutenant Hall: 'They're Catholics. It's a Catholic house…' Lieutenant Hall said to me: 'How do

> you know this, Corporal J?' When I'd entered the living room I'd noticed a picture of the Sacred Heart. This was hung on the wall. My mother would have crossed herself at the picture. The Catholic school I'd been to as a youngster had drummed all this into me. Yet now to me it was a sign of who the enemy was: Catholics meant IRA.[4]

Nicky Curtis was in the Green Howards' regiment and was sent to Northern Ireland in 1970.

> I already had bonds with Ireland. My father's forefathers had been Irish and, raised Catholic, my spiritual grounding was there. So it was a very different feeling for me to be going there rather than the alien cultures of the Caribbean or the Far East that I had visited in the past. This time I didn't feel like a visitor, or an invader, but more like a returning 'natural' coming back to help out. My sympathies were with the Catholics because of the denial of their basic constitutional right to vote through the 'no house – no vote' system.[5]

On his first day in Northern Ireland, Curtis arrived in Belfast.

> Suddenly I was shocked by something that would haunt me for years – an incredible, surging feeling of déja vu. Even though I'd never been to Ireland before, in this moment it felt like a homecoming. It was a strange mixture, of newness and yet something worryingly familiar. With my grandma being a classic, flame-haired Irish Catholic, I was used to the accent and tales of the old country, but nothing that prepared me for this.[6]

'With the Catholic community having more to fight for… I found myself in the dilemma of understanding them and yet, at the same time, [was] increasingly horrified by the their methods,' he recalled.[7]

Curtis knew, and had in fact trained (but was no relation to) Robert Curtis, the first British soldier killed in Northern Ireland during the modern Troubles. Another contemporary was thc mysterious Robert Nairac. Curtis mistakenly believed – as did many – that Nairac was second generation Irish. 'Like me, he had been raised as a devout Catholic and, like me, he had gone through the same feelings upon landing in Northern Ireland for the first time, his knowledge of the conflict's history giving him the belief he might be able to do some good,' said Curtis.[8]

It would appear that while Nairac was not a child of the diaspora, he often claimed he was – to Irish people, and to his British Army colleagues. He had been brought up a Catholic and knew more than the average British soldier about Irish history, but there is little evidence to show he was in any sense Irish. Nairac went to the posh Catholic private school Ampleforth, and as a schoolboy apparently wanted to emulate T. E. Lawrence, the Anglo-Irish maverick British soldier and spy. Like Lawrence, he studied history at Oxford and was recruited into military intelligence.[9]

Nairac spent boyhood summers in Ireland with friends and after Sandhurst did a postgraduate course at university in Dublin. Nairac's self-appointed Irishness bewildered and worried some of his soldier colleagues. One said: ' I was able to discover and understand to a degree some of his weaknesses in the strong Catholic belief he had. He had a very strong and curious affinity, in the strangest possible way, towards the IRA… He told me that during his college days he had boxed Martin Mcchan, later to become an IRA leader of some notoriety.'[10]

A former girlfriend described him as 'like a man obsessed; he told me that evening that because he was a Catholic and because he was in the Army, he felt he could personally bring the two sides together.'[11]

Nairac was apparently fearless in going into republican heartlands to pick up intelligence in pubs and clubs, and felt confident that he could pass as local. He believed he had mastered several Ulster accents and was often seen socialising with locals in Catholic neighbourhoods. 'It's okay,' he told a colleague. 'They think I'm Irish. I'm one of the boys.' One south Armagh republican said Nairac 'was a good-looking fellow who would even try to chat up the girls in Cross[maglen] and spin yarns about how his mother was from Galway'.[12]

But Nairac's disguise was ultimately unconvincing. One Saturday night in May 1977 he went to a pub in Drumintee, Armagh, called the Three Steps Inn. It was known as a republican pub, so Nairac took an enormous risk going there. It is believed he was hoping to meet a contact who had indicated he might act as an informer. Nairac pretended he was Danny McErlaine, a republican from Belfast. A band was playing in the pub, and Nairac – whose undercover style was audacious rather than understated – went up and sang two IRA songs. Something about Nairac's appearance tipped off some customers and he was challenged about his identity. Whatever happened next, it appears that a few men bundled Nairac out of the pub and into the car park; he was never seen again. Although two men were convicted of Nairac's murder, his body was never found. Predictably – because a corpse was never discovered – several theories are still floated about what really happened to Nairac, including one that he took the whole Irish identity thing too seriously, really did go over to the IRA and is alive and well somewhere in Ireland. Some loyalists, claimed Curtis, believe this to be true.[13]

Bert Henshaw undertook six emergency tours of Northern Ireland between 1969 and 1977 with the First Battalion of the Royal Green Jackets. He grew up in Liverpool and until the age of eleven lived with his grandmother, a Protestant from the south of Ireland. He recalled that the 'highlight of our year was watching the Orange Lodge walk past in July, when our grandmother, a staunch supporter of the local lodge, would give us Union flags to wave.'[14]

On his first tour Henshaw was sent to Belfast. 'When we went onto the barricades on the Falls Road the vigilantes were singing rebel songs, and were amazed when I started to join in. I'd learned them all as a kid in Liverpool,' he said.[15]

James [last name withheld] of the Royal Artillery was sent to Derry in 1973 and Belfast the following year. During one raid 'we arrested a leading republican, you know the bearded fellow, who's now involved in negotiations with the British government,' he said. 'My grandfather came from Letterkenny, and many of the people I stopped and questioned in Derry had the same surname as me… I began to wonder if I was interrogating distant cousins,' he said.[16]

Bernard O'Mahoney was born in England in 1960 of Irish parents and brought up Catholic.

> I never felt English growing up, although I suppose I never felt properly Irish either. I knew my roots were in Ireland and I felt comfortable around Irish people. In a sense I lived in an Irish world… I spent every summer holiday in Ireland, and I loved being there, especially with my mother's family in Sligo. My maternal grandfather, Tom, held republican views.[17]

O'Mahoney had troubled teenage years involving petty crime, violence and increasingly regular contact with the police. Although he grew up in the English midlands, the Irish Troubles repeatedly intruded on his life. His brother was employed to clean up the rubble of the Birmingham pub bombings in November 1974. While O'Mahoney admired the courage of the bombers in taking such risks in planting explosives, the incident did nothing to nurture any republican stirrings in him. 'In fact, it had turned me completely against the IRA – the effect it had on a lot of one-time republican sympathisers – and I hoped the perpetrators would themselves die horribly. However, for all that, I still couldn't regard them as cowards…,' he said.[18]

O'Mahoney had 'a cousin who served a prison sentence for rioting in Belfast in the early seventies. On his release he came to live with us in Codsall for six months,' he said.[19]

O'Mahoney decided to join the British Army to escape the spiral of crime he was sinking into. He deliberately chose to enlist in an Irish regiment because at that time they were not sent to Northern Ireland. But after he'd joined the 5th Royal Inniskilling Dragoon Guards the rules changed, and his regiment was the first Irish one to be sent to Northern Ireland. O'Mahoney said the British military authorities asked him if – in view of his heritage – he wanted to be excused the tour of duty, but he decided he'd rather stick with his friends. He was sent to patrol Fermanagh the day after IRA hunger striker Bobby Sands was elected as the local MP in April 1981.

The British Army has since denied any policy of excusing second generation Irish soldiers tours of duty in Northern Ireland. Captain Dale Clarke RA, Directorate of Corporate Communications (Army), explained the official British military line that 'prior to 1981, and indeed since at least 1993, there had been a policy by which no such Regiment (ie one that recruited extensively in Northern and Southern Ireland) undertook operational duties in Ireland. The primary problems of deploying such units to Ireland following the establishment of the Irish Free State, and subsequently the Republic of Ireland, clearly related both to the wider political issues and to the personal issue for those personnel involved,' he claimed.[20]

Clarke recounted that

> this policy was reviewed on a number of occasions after 1969, but that the concerns regarding the situation in Northern Ireland prior to the late-1970's precluded any changes in this policy. The matter came under discussion again in 1978/79 and resulted in a paper being raised for consideration before the Executive Committee of the Army Board (ECAB). This resulted in a proposal that the deployment of Irish-named Royal Armoured Corps (RAC) Regiments might be viable and that, what might be termed an 'experimental tour', might take place in 1981. It was agreed that this proposal should be pursued and this resulted in the 5th Inniskilling Dragoon Guards tour in the Fermanagh area of April-August 1981.
>
> Prior to 1988/89 the only other tour by an Irish-named Regiment was a Squadron of the Queen's Royal Hussars, who undertook Prison Guard Force duties at The Maze in 1983-84. The first tour by one of the two Irish-named infantry regiments did not take place until September 1988, when 1 Royal Irish were sent to the Province. I should point

> out that individual members of Irish-named Regiments undertook service in Northern Ireland prior to the decision to allow their units to do so and will have done so, on an individual basis, since that time. Such duties would have been on the basis of undertaking specific postings or individuals, or groups of individuals, being attached and serving with other units. Moreover, many other men of Irish parentage, serving with units that had no specific Irish connections, will also have served in the Province.

Clarke claimed he was 'not aware of any specific "opt-out" being provided for in the case of Irish-named Regiments. The units would have been deployed as a whole and the case for excluding any individual from such a tour would have been considered on the merits of each case. It is clear that some personnel were specifically excluded from undertaking a tour of Northern Ireland for security reasons, either due to their assessment following screening on enlistment or security screening undertaken prior to the tour.'

Whatever the official position on second generation soldiers, O'Mahoney found himself in a hostile Northern Ireland in 1981. Soon after arriving he was part of a British Army detail that raided a republican suspect's house.

> The inside was tidy, but spartan. A woman stood in the front room. Her two boys, aged about eight and ten, stood next to her with their arms around her… One of the boys looked at me. I smiled instinctively. But he didn't respond; all he could see was my rifle and British uniform… I looked around and noticed Jesus Christ looking down on us all from a large wooden crucifix on the wall… I left the house feeling deflated and uneasy. It was at those times I felt like a Judas for betraying my own kind.[21]

The tension of living in cramped quarters began to produce strains. Many of his soldier colleagues were Protestants from Northern Ireland, uncertain how to react to his Irish Catholic parentage. '[One of them] would say to me: "Hiya Fenian!"

I would tell him to fuck off, which would make him laugh "Ha! Ha! Ha!" he would cackle, as if we were best friends joshing. I hated the bastard.'[22]

The attitudes of some of the Protestant squaddies became an increasingly difficult issue for O'Mahoney. 'When in their company I often felt that if I'd been brought up a Catholic alongside them I would probably have ended up stalking the countryside with a black balaclava and kalashnikov hoping to shoot them,' he said.[23]

O'Mahoney eventually started going out with a girl in the Ulster Defence Regiment, and despite many cultural difficulties (including lying to her mother about his ancestry), O'Mahoney was keen enough to stay in Northern Ireland that he applied to join the UDR too. His application was successful but he found that some of his girlfriend's friends 'did not accept me. My blood tainted me; and even my prospective UDR uniform could not redeem me'.[24]

He eventually split up with his girlfriend, and moved back to England. 'With my Irish blood and English upbringing I should have felt at home there [in Northern Ireland]. But I had never felt, and would never feel, so alien,' he said.[25]

There were also police officers with apparently Irish backgrounds whose job it was to interrogate republican suspects. Detective Inspector Timothy Blake denied ever having interrogated Gerry Conlon in Guildford police station, but Conlon insists Blake assaulted him during questioning about the Guildford pub bombings.

> Blake grabbed me by the balls and squeezed them really hard. I was screaming with pain and when he let go I fell to the floor-only to be lifted up by the hair. I was again put against the wall… Again, Blake grabbed me by the balls and squeezed. I was crying, in pain and confused. I started to lose all sense of time.[26]

'Blake had these staring eyes,' said Conlon. 'He told me he was a Catholic from an Irish family, but evil murdering bastards like me made him sick.' Blake was adamant at the Guildford Four trial that he had not assaulted Conlon or Paul Hill, who both claimed he had. He denied having questioned Conlon at all, and had some difficulty explaining how, if they had not met, Conlon knew he was a Catholic. 'Blake, it was subsequently discovered, had fabricated notes of interviews which, fortunately, he was too arrogant or stupid to destroy,' Hill wrote after his conviction was quashed and when official accounts of his interrogation and the interrogation of the others were found to have been doctored by the police.[27]

Some convicted republicans discovered their jailers had Irish backgrounds. Paddy Kelly, sentenced to 20 years in 1997 for conspiracy to cause explosions in London, said he found that

> in jail in England the screws with Irish names felt they had to be harsher. When I was sentenced in Full Sutton [Prison], I was asking some black prisoners and they found the same thing with black screws – that they had to be tougher than the white screws to prove themselves. The Irish-named screws were particularly nasty – I never found any of them nice, except one woman who just did her job. The rest went out of their way to be nasty pieces of work. They had to prove themselves to be worse. The ordinary English screws were fine, just did their job.[28]

Kelly spoke to them about their sense of identity. 'They'd say some of their families came over in the Famine, and some of them said didn't know [about their Irishness], and some of them obviously didn't like their Irish names. A lot of them had come from the military,' he said.[29]

Other second generation Irish people born in Britain were spectacularly violent to Catholics they suspected of being republican sympathisers. Loyalist paramilitary Michael Stone became internationally famous when television pictures showed him attacking a republican funeral with hand grenades in 1988. In March of that year, three unarmed IRA members had been killed by an SAS unit in Gibraltar. Stone approached the mourners at their funeral in Milltown Cemetery in Belfast before firing into the crowd and throwing grenades at those near the coffins. Three people were killed in the attack, and more injured. Stone was captured as he fled the scene, and confessed to several more killings during his years as a loyalist paramilitary.

Although Stone was from a long loyalist tradition on his father's side, and his great-grandfather had signed the 1912 Covenant in blood to show how far he was prepared to go to prevent Home Rule for Ireland, Stone's mother was called Mary Bridget Sullivan, and Stone was in fact born in Harborne, Birmingham in 1955.[29]

Stone's parents split up when he was a baby, and his father took him to Belfast. He was reared by an aunt and uncle, whom he believed to be his parents, and only told the truth when he was at primary school. His mother, he said, was 'an unmentioned subject'. Stone said 'I knew I was truly British. I was, after all, English and my father served in the Royal Corps of Signals. Maybe my mother was Catholic but my father was Protestant and I was raised in the Protestant faith.' Despite a *Sunday World* story in 1988 claiming Stone had been baptised a Catholic, his biographer Martin Dillon confirmed there is no evidence to substantiate the claim.[30]

Other second generation paramilitaries who fought the IRA came from within their own ranks. Kerry native Eamon Collins left the IRA and turned informer. His book *Killing Rage* ought to be treated with the suspicion of any evidence produced by a paid supergrass. The book claims a second generation IRA recruit – Mickey – was active in Newry in the 1980s but decided to switch sides.

> Mickey's parents had met in England, where Mickey was born and brought up… His father brought the family back to Northern Ireland when Mickey was in his teens, so Mickey retained a Manchester accent, supported Manchester United and even returned to Manchester University to study for his degree in languages.[31]

Mickey, according to Collins, embarked on a killing spree during the 1980s which included shooting a former policeman, a former UDR soldier, two policemen and a Catholic man in a betting shop he mistook for an RUC detective. 'I could not help thinking of Mickey's English mother, and his own upbringing in England,' said Collins. 'The vicious zealot was nothing more than an adoptive nationalist trying to be more Irish than the Irish themselves.' But Mickey, claimed Collins, was sent into exile by the IRA after also turning informer.[32]

As informers, police officers, prison warders, paramilitaries and British soldiers, second generation Irish people in Britain played significant roles in the war against the IRA. Some were uneasy with their British allegiance, and felt they were betraying their heritage by fighting republicans. Others were unswervingly loyal to the Crown. The most powerful second generation figure of the Troubles has been British Prime Minister Tony Blair.

> Ireland is in my blood. My mother was born in the flat above her grandmother's hardware shop in the main street of Ballyshannon in Donegal… It was there in the seas off the Irish coast that I learned to swim and my father took me to my first pub, a remote little house in the country for a Guinness, a taste I have never forgotten and which is always a pleasure to repeat.[23]

Blair's second generation heritage has not resulted in any hankering for a united Ireland, or sympathy for republicanism. His first official visit outside London after being elected Prime Minister in May 1997 was to Northern Ireland, and the Royal Ulster Agricultural Show. He assured his audience he had no doubt about how to deal with the IRA – 'any shred of justification terrorists might have claimed for violence has long since disappeared,' he said. 'The police and armed forces will continue to bring their full weight to bear on the men of violence.' He confirmed the union with Britain was safe in his hands. 'A political settlement is not a slippery slope to a united Ireland. The government will not be persuaders for unity. Unionism should have more confidence in itself and its future… None of us in this hall today, even the youngest, is likely to see Northern Ireland as anything but a part of the United Kingdom,' he said. [34]

13.
Faith of Our Fathers

Imagine for a moment Irish republicanism without its second generation figures. How would the 1916 Rising have looked without Connolly or Clarke? Would it have happened at all? Imagine the War for Independence without de Valera. Even Michael Collins, though born in Cork, was in a real sense a London republican. He spent most of his adult life in the city and without a unit of the London Volunteers, where would Collins have joined? How would Fianna Fáil have been established without de Valera, or the Provisional IRA founded without MacStiofáin?

Nor did second generation republicanism start in 1916. The celebrated Fenian O'Donovan Rossa mentions several English-born Fenian prisoners in jail with him in the 1860s, including John O'Brien, who – Rossa explained – left his job as a druggist's clerk in his native London to go to Ireland and 'enlist in a regiment there so he could teach love of country to the Irish who were also in it.' And in Millbank Prison with Rossa too was the English-born Edward Pillsworth St Clair, son of an Irish troop-sergeant in the British Army. St Clair was sentenced to ten years penal servitude for his Fenian agitation in the British Army, and was involved in a failed escape attempt from the jail with the famous John Devoy.[1]

Those second generation Irish republicans who fought in 1916 and the following years have largely been ignored by history, despite their crucial contribution to Ireland. Brian O'Higgins wrote 50 years later:

> Sometimes it is forgotten that men of Irish birth or of Irish descent (some of them had never seen Ireland before) came home from England and Scotland to prepare for and take part in the Rising. They were from London, Liverpool, Manchester, Glasgow and many other centres, and there were a few who never saw their homes again. They began to arrive in Dublin in the early part of 1916 and went into camp at Larkfield, Kimmage, where they drilled and trained every day up to Easter. Raids were made for them afterwards in the jails and in Frongoch Camp by the British, who held they were liable for service in England's army under the Conscription Act, but their comrades stood by them to the last and there was many a battle of wits over them. Some who were found underwent incredible punishment when attempts were made to put them into khaki, but not even one gave in. The record of the exiles at Easter, 1916, is an honourable one.[2]

Honourable or not, the legacy of the Volunteers from London and elsewhere in Britain has left an indelible imprint on the course of Irish history. Joe Good, the Cockney who signed up with London Volunteers with his friend Michael Collins, at first declined to participate in the Civil War, but entered on the Free State side on hearing of Collins' death. Ambushed and captured by the IRA, Good was about to be shot dead when the republican commander leading the ambush, the legendary Dan Breen, stepped forward, recognised him as a 1916 man, and spared his life. Good settled into a quiet civilian life after the Civil War. He stayed in Ireland, married a London-Irish girl, and had four children. He was an enthusiastic gardener in his Dublin home in Templeogue, and married the poet Pamela Heal when his wife died. Good's son Maurice said his father's accent 'was his own invention… Churchillian, but with an Irish cadence.' Good died of emphysema, aged 67, in 1962.

He had rarely participated in commemorations about 1916, and Maurice recounted that as a Dublin schoolboy he 'won a lot of sixpences by bringing many a doubting Tom, Dick and Paddy to the 1916 room at the National Museum and showing them my father in the official group photograph of the survivors of the GPO garrison. My schoolmates were also slow to believe that so many of the men had been born in England, but I could point to their names at the bottom of the photograph.'[3]

That so many Dublin schoolboys were ignorant of the part played by the Kimmage garrison in the Easter Rising is not so perplexing, despite the emphasis on the history of the birth of the state in those first decades after independence. While rousing books were published around the country celebrating local contributions to the war for independence, like *Kerry's Fighting Story 1916-21* and *Rebel Cork's Fighting Story*, and songs like *How the Boys from the County Cork Beat up the Black and Tans* and *The Belfast Brigade* and *The Drumboe Martyrs* reminded Ireland of the courage of specific localities and their IRA heroes, no one wrote books or songs about the Volunteers from Britain. Irish communities in London or Glasgow did not keep the memory of local republicans alive the way they did in Tralee or Clonakilty. No one published a pamphlet on *The London-Irish Fighting Story*, and the contribution of British-born Volunteers was very quickly consigned to obscurity.

Another of the Cockneys in the museum photograph was Johnny 'Blimey' O'Connor, who had fought on the republican side during the Civil War. On hearing of Good's death he rushed to Dublin and arranged a military funeral for his former comrade and adversary.

Margaret Skinnider, the only female republican casualty of the 1916 Rising, recovered from her bullet wounds and toured the US to rally support for Irish independence. She fought on the anti-treaty side in the Civil War, and was paymaster of the IRA until her arrest in 1923. Prominent in the Irish trade union movement throughout her life, she died in 1971.

Sean Nunan, one of the brothers from Brixton in the GPO during Easter week, went on to a distinguished career in the foreign service of the new Irish state. He was in the Irish Commission to London at the outbreak of the Second World War, and later in the 1940s was Irish ambassador to the US.

Liverpudlian John Pinkman, who joined the Liverpool IRA in 1920 and then the Free State Army, left Ireland soon after the Civil War ended. He spent several decades travelling the world, survived the Battle of the Atlantic as a merchant seaman and settled in the US. He returned to Ireland in 1955, worked for Dublin Corporation and died, aged 68, in 1970. He too was given a full military funeral.

Edward Casey, the young London-Irish boy who joined the British Army and had a colourful military career, was unsurprisingly among the first to be discharged at the end of the First World War. He emigrated to New Zealand the following year, and wrote the account of his army life sometime later. It is held in London's Imperial War Museum.

Other second generation figures who fought between 1916 and 1923, and their children and grandchildren, form an impressive list of those who played prominent roles in the formation of independent Ireland.

John MacBride, executed as one of the 1916 leaders, passed his republican values to his son Seán, who fought on the anti-treaty side in the Civil War and was briefly Chief of Staff of the IRA in the late 1930s. Although he left the IRA before the bombing campaign of England began in 1939, he continued to provide legal representation to IRA prisoners in Ireland. In December 1939 he successfully argued in the High Court that the act under which IRA members were being held was unconstitutional, a decision which resulted in 53 internees being freed. In 1946, IRA prisoner Seán McCaughey died after a hunger and thirst strike in an attempt to force the authorities to grant him political status. MacBride had been his legal counsel, and at the inquest into his death MacBride exposed the conditions in which republican prisoners were being held. In one celebrated exchange with the prison doctor he asked 'You would not keep a dog in conditions like that, would you, doctor?' to which the doctor agreed that he wouldn't.[4]

MacBride entered constitutional politics in the 1940s, and established a new republican party, Clann na Poblachta. The party enjoyed initial – if brief – success, and helped form a coalition government in 1948. MacBride became Minister for External Affairs, and it was this government that declared Ireland a Republic.

During the 1950s MacBride recommenced his legal practice, and then took up a post as Secretary General of the International Commission of Jurists in Geneva. He co-founded Amnesty International in 1961, and became United Nations Commissioner for Namibia. He advised the IRA delegation led by Seán MacStiofáin which met with British government representatives in 1972. His reputation as an international statesman and humanitarian grew, and he was awarded the Nobel Peace Prize in 1974, and the Lenin International Peace Prize in 1977.

When a book of prison writings by IRA hunger striker Bobby Sands was published a year after his death (1982), it was MacBride who wrote the 15-page introduction, outlining the history of republican resistance to British rule in Northern Ireland since 1921. 'The death of Bobby Sands and his writings are but a fall-out resulting from the cruel interference by Britain in the affairs of the Irish nation,' he wrote.[5] By the time MacBride himself died in early 1988 he was one of the most respected human rights advocates in the world.

James Connolly's daughter, Nora Connolly O'Brien, was born in Scotland. In 1903 her family emigrated to the United States where she worked as a milliner. They moved to Belfast in 1907 where she worked in the mills, founded the Young Republicans Party and the Belfast Branch of Cumann na mBan. In 1914, while working for the Irish Transport and General Workers' Union in Dublin, she took part in the Howth gun-running operation which armed the Irish Volunteers. In early 1916 she accompanied Liam Mellows from England after he had escaped from Reading Gaol, and during the 1916 Rising she smuggled dispatches from Padraig Pearse to the Belfast Volunteers. After the Rising Connolly O'Brien travelled to America, disguised as a priest, to update the Irish American organisation Clann na Gael of the situation in Ireland. In late 1917 she returned to Ireland via England after an order barring her from Ireland had been issued.

Connolly O'Brien worked for the ITGWU while campaigning for Sinn Féin in the 1918 general election. She married Seamus O'Brien in 1922 and, in 1923, when Margaret Skinnider was arrested, Connolly O'Brien replaced her as Paymaster-General of the IRA. She was imprisoned by the Free State in Mountjoy Gaol, the North Dublin Union and later in Kilmainham Gaol. In 1926 Connolly O'Brien became a member of the Irish Senate and sat for three terms. She remained a lifelong republican and took part in political debates and H-Block support rallies until shortly before her death in 1981.

Accounts of the 1916 Rising have often centred on the importance of Padraig Pearse, and he is usually credited with being the first President of the Republic. It was he who wrote the bulk of the Proclamation and he who read it out on the pavement outside the GPO. But the history of Pearse's part in the Rising has been written at the expense of Thomas Clarke. Clarke was the most senior of the republicans, the first name on the Proclamation. His wife Kathleen asked him if this meant he was the first President of the Republic. 'Yes, that's what it means,' said Clarke. She asked him if, in the event of the Rising being successful, he would act as President. 'If we win through it will take a long time. By then I fear I would be physically unable for the job, but if I am fit I shall certainly act. I have more knowledge and experience of our enemy, and if necessary the force and ruthlessness needed for the position,' he told her.[6]

After his capture, as he waited in Kilmainham Jail to be executed, Clarke told his wife Kathleen how, when they had arrived outside the GPO that Easter Monday, he as President had shot the lock from the door and led the charge into the building. According to Kathleen Clarke: 'The other men who had accompanied him, four of them signatories to the Proclamation, MacDermott, Plunkett, Connolly and Pearse, fell back a step for him to do this. In this way, he was first into the GPO'. Clarke and his widow were not alone in believing him to be the first President. In June 1917, when the last of the republican prisoners were released from jails in England, Kathleen Clarke went to meet the train bringing them to Dublin. 'Seán McGarry was the first I recognised,' she said. 'His wife and family were standing with me. When his welcome to them was over he turned to me and said, "Who the hell made Pearse President?"'[7]

Ironically, the station where Kathleen Clarke met Seán McGarry – Westland Row – was renamed Pearse Station in 1966. One of Dublin's main roads is also named after Pearse, but no such tributes have been made to Clarke in the city. Today St. Enda's, Pearse's school in the south Dublin suburb of Rathfarnham, is an impressive museum carefully preserved for visitors to study Pearse's life and work. In contrast, the city's commemoration of Clarke is a small plaque embedded on the outside wall of his old shop at 75a Parnell Street. It states simply: 'This Building Was Formerly The Tobacco Shop of THOMAS CLARKE (Fenian) First Signatory To The 1916 Proclamation Executed 3rd May 1916.' Compared to the tributes made to honour Pearse, it is not much of a monument.

Ironically, Tom Clarke's birthplace, Hurst Park military hospital on the Isle of Wight, became the site of Parkhurst Prison, where many republicans were jailed during the Troubles. In June 1974, IRA prisoner Michael Gaughan died after 65 days on hunger strike in a bid for political status at the prison.

Eamon de Valera dominated Ireland's first 50 years in a way unmatched by any other political figure. He was President of Ireland 1959-1973; Taoiseach 1937-1948, 1951-1954, and 1957-1959; President of the Executive Council of the Irish Free State 1932-1937; President of the first Dáil 1919-1921; and President of the second Dáil 1921-January 1922. His grand-daughter Síle de Valera has carved an impressive political career in recent decades. First elected as a TD in 1977, when she became its youngest member, she was a Member of the European Parliament from 1979 to 1984 and has held various significant party and state portfolios, including Vice-President of Fianna Fáil and Minister of State at the Department of Education and Science.

De Valera's grandson Éamon Ó Cuív was also a minister in the Fianna Fáil coalition government that came to power in 2002, becoming Minister for Community, Rural and Gaeltacht Affairs. Ó Cuív, known as Dev Og ['Young Dev'] in some quarters because of his striking resemblance to his famous grandfather, represents Fianna Fáil for Galway West.

Eamon de Valera's Civil War comrade Erskine Childers was executed by the Free State in November 1922. His son, also called Erskine, was born in London in 1905 and went to an English school and university. In 1932 he moved to Ireland and became advertising manager of the Fianna Fáil – supporting *Irish Press* newspaper. He was elected to the Dáil several times as a Fianna Fáil TD and held several senior cabinet posts, including Minister for Transport and Power, Minister for Health and Tánaiste.

He stood in the election for President of Ireland in May 1973 as the Fianna Fáil candidate and won, becoming the country's fourth president and succeeding de Valera in the post. He died suddenly in Dublin, on November 17, 1974, from coronary thrombosis.

Desmond Fitzgerald, born and brought up in London, moved to Ireland some years before the Rising and organised the Dingle Volunteers. He was in charge of food supplies in the GPO during the Rising, and became an important figure in the Free State government. His son Garret was Taoiseach from June 1981 to March 1982 (a period during which ten republican hunger strikers died in Northern Ireland), and again from later in 1982 to 1987. Garret Fitzgerald followed a hard line on negotiations with the IRA, and while Taoiseach in September 1981 wrote that 'the sooner the IRA gains can be wiped out, the better. I appreciate the

IRA are a threat to our government, to our democracy, and not a threat to Britain. It's we who have to live with them. It is we who have to fight them and save democracy here.'[8]

Alarmed at republican electoral success in 1981 and 1983, Fitzgerald attempted to shore up the constitutional nationalist party, the SDLP, by brokering an agreement with the British government. 'The rapid rise in the Sinn Féin vote to form one-third of the total nationalist vote made an eventual majority for nationalism in the North seem conceivable, and the IRA might then be emboldened to raise the level of violence to the point at which it provoked a civil war, endangering the security of the whole island,' he claimed.

> This danger led the government in which I was Taoiseach to abandon for the time being attempts to seek an agreement with the Unionists – then a somewhat illusory goal in any event given repeated Unionist rejections of moves towards a power-sharing arrangement in the North – and to seek an agreement instead with the British government that would revive nationalist confidence in constitutional methods, and thus win back support from Sinn Féin, to the advantage of the SDLP. Despite the failure of Margaret Thatcher's government to implement fully the security aspect of the resulting Anglo-Irish Agreement, political support for Sinn Féin fell in its wake from one-third to well below one-quarter of the nationalist vote in the North. And this in time led the IRA to rethink its 'Armalite and ballot-box' strategy, and then to the ceasefire of 1994.[9]

Fitzgerald saw little connection between his father's actions in the IRA and the more recent Troubles, and said '…it is unhistorical to see the tragic events in the North as having been mainly inspired by memories of 1916. Although 1916 has certainly been used as a justification for the IRA's campaign of violence, that campaign has been much more a continuation of an endemic tradition of pogroms and sectarianism in the north-east, the roots of which lie far back in the history of that part of Ireland in the 19th century – indeed right back to the 17th century.'[10]

In their own ways, second generation figures from Tom Clarke to Seán MacStiofáin to Tony Blair all tried to end the centuries-old conflict. The latest attempt at peace has been made possible, in a very real sense, by two Irish-Americans, Bill Flynn and Chuck Feeney. Flynn, a New York insurance executive, is second generation Irish with a father from Loughisland in County Down and a mother from Mayo. In 1991, Flynn met two representatives from Noraid, an Irish reepublican fundraising group in the US. He told them he could not support the use of violence, but 'I told them I was totally supportive of the concept of Ireland getting unified. My parents before me, my relatives were all of one mind on that,' he said.[11] Challenged by the Noraid men about what exactly he was doing to bring about a united Ireland, Flynn travelled to Belfast to see Gerry Adams to explore ways he might be able to help.

Flynn and fellow businessman Chuck Feeney, whose family came from Fermanagh, undertook a series of exploratory initiatives aimed at breaking new ground in the debate on the conflict. 'In our private meeting with Sinn Féin I said I, and corporate America in general, felt embarrassed and humiliated by the use of violence and could never support it. I said the time had come, in furtherance of their cause, to lay aside arms,' said Flynn.[12]

In January 1994 Flynn, in his capacity as chairman of the prestigious National Committee on Foreign Policy, invited Gerry Adams and other politicians to a one-day conference in New York to discuss the conflict. Members of the Irish diaspora in the US, notably Senator Edward Kennedy and his sister Jean Kennedy Smith (by then US Ambassador in Dublin) lobbied hard for Adams to be granted a visa to attend the conference. The British government was apoplectic that Adams might be allowed to travel to the US while the IRA's warfare continued. The US State Department too was against the visa, but President Clinton, pushed hard by the Irish diaspora, agreed to allow Adams into the US to attend Flynn's conference. The visa incident became a key event in securing an eventual IRA ceasefire and unlocking the forces that would eventually generate a peace process.

Flynn also made important overtures to the loyalist leadership, and was brought into the confidence of many leading loyalist politicians. Before the Combined Loyalist Military Command announced its historic ceasefire in October 1994, the paramilitary leaders had told Flynn in advance what they were going to do. They even invited him over from the US for the announcement. He sat out of sight in a back room, away from the media, as the ceasefire was announced to the world. 'I was the only Catholic invited,' he said. 'The only nationalist or republican.'[13]

Flynn, Feeney and other Irish-Americans played a significant part in facilitating the series of talks that eventually led to the Good Friday Agreement. Flynn's contribution to ending the Troubles stands as one of the great second generation achievements in Irish history. The Good Friday Agreement, ratified by the electorate on both sides of the border, has provided a basis for the end of the modern conflict. The Agreement also sought to reposition the legal definition of Irishness.

Being Irish in a legal sense, as most second generation people know, rests on one's ability to pass the citizenship test. Since the foundation of the Irish state, there has always been a clear legal basis for Irish citizenship. Article 3 of the Irish Free State Constitution provided citizenship to those resident in the state on the date the Constitution came into force, December 6, 1922, once they (or one of their parents) was born there or they had resided within the Irish Free State for not less than seven years previously. In 1935, the Irish Nationality and Citizenship Act was passed, which provided for citizenship by birth or descent.[14]

This was followed by the 1956 Irish Nationality and Citizenship Act, section 6(1) of which states that 'Every person born in Ireland is an Irish citizen from birth'. And then Article 2 of the Constitution, as amended by the Good Friday Agreement, reaffirms the birthright of every person born on the island of Ireland to be part of the Irish nation, which includes citizenship unless they are otherwise precluded by law.

Most second generation Irish people know they have a right to be Irish, to live and work in Ireland, because at least one of their parents was born in Ireland. But what of the rights of parents of Irish citizens? In 1981 Mr Fajujonu, a Moroccan national, and his wife, arrived in Ireland as illegal immigrants. After eight years residence, Mr Fajujonu was instructed by the Irish government to leave the state. The Fajujonus took their case to court and successfully argued that because they had given birth to an Irish born child (in fact three, but only one was the subject of court proceedings with her parents) the immediate family had the right to remain in Ireland. In reaching its conclusions, the Supreme Court held that, as an Irish citizen, the Fajujonu daughter was entitled to reside in Ireland. Also, as a citizen, she had the constitutional right to the company of her family. In the absence of compelling circumstances, the family could not be deported.

But then in January 2003 the Irish Supreme Court declared that non-Irish parents who had given birth to children in Ireland had no automatic right to stay in Ireland. The case centred on the claims of the Lobe family from the Czech Republic and the Osayande family from Nigeria, who had both sought asylum in Ireland in the first half of 2001. The court found that while their children were Irish citizens, having been born in Ireland, their non-Irish parents could be deported.

Quite how these first generation Irish people will eventually see their identity, and what they will make of the country that offered them citizenship but deported their parents, remains to be seen.

How second generation status will develop in the coming years cannot be known yet either. In just over a decade Ireland will be celebrating the centenary of the Easter Rising. Perhaps reflections on the previous century will prompt a proper recognition of the parts played by figures like 'Blimey' O'Connor, the Nunan brothers and Margaret Skinnider in establishing the state.

And if the war in Northern Ireland really has ended by 2016, it might be easier to identify yourself as second generation Irish in

Britain than it has been since 1970. While many second generation Irish people might not have regarded the Irish conflict as having had a huge impact on their lives, some – like Michael Stone – were virtually born into the Troubles, while others – like Seán MacStiofáin – chose to join the Troubles and others still – like the Maguire children – had the Troubles thrust upon them.

Without further armed conflict in the north, the second generation experience in Britain might more closely mirror that in the US, where it has been far less awkward or uncomfortable to take sides or to publicly define and explain your identity. By 2016, it might even be as socially acceptable to be Irish-Scottish or Irish-English as it is to be Irish-American. First generation Irish exasperation at foreign-born cousins insisting on claiming an Irish identity might even have mellowed into a more tolerant definition of Irish identity. 'I don't know why everyone I meet has to tell me where his father and mother come from in Ireland,' wrote an irritated Frank McCourt about second generation Irish people in New York, which is a touch rich coming from a Manhattan-born writer.[15]

Perhaps in the Ireland of 2016 children of the diaspora will at last be accepted as properly Irish, as welcome into the parlour as Timothy or Pat, and the insecure Plastic Paddy image will have been crushed and recycled into a confident, modern and authentic Irishness.

Endnotes

Chapter 1

1. Mary J. Hickman 'Locating the Irish Diaspora,' *Irish Journal of Sociology*, Vol II, No. 2, 2002, p. 16
2. Mary J. Hickman, Sarah Morgan and Bronwen Walter, *Second-Generation Irish People in Britain: a demographic, socio-economic and health profile* (Irish Studies Centre, University of North London, June 2001), pp. 12-13. The authors also identify other possible ways to categorise people with an Irish parent-in the US, for example, some sociologists use the category of '1.5 generation' to describe people born elsewhere who arrive between the ages of 6-13, whereas those who arrive before the age of six get a 1.75 generation mark, and those who settle in the new country between 13 and 17 are allocated 1.25. These subdivisions are unnecessarily complicated for the purposes of this book.
3. Catherine Jackson, 'Census Figures Boost Irish,' *Irish Post* February 22, 2003
4. www.apc/Irish2.co.uk
5. S. Harding and R. Balarajan , 'Patterns of mortality in second generation Irish living in England and Wales', *British Medical Journal* 312:1389-1392, quoted in Mary J Hickman, Sarah Morgan and Bronwen Walter, op. cit., p.39. For educational level attainment see pp. 22-29.
6. S. Harding, 'The health of the second generation Irish living in England and Wales,' in *The Health of the Irish in Britain: a report of a community conference* (London: Federation of Irish Societies, 1998), quoted in Mary J Hickman, Sarah Morgan, Bronwen Walter, op. cit., p. 39
7. 'More Young Men Dying', BBC News Online, February 16, 1999, report of ONS figures.
8. Mary J Hickman, Sarah Morgan and Bronwen Walter, op. cit., p. 40
9. Robert Kee, *Trial and Error* (Hamish Hamilton, London 1986) p. 97
10. Judith Ward appeal transcript, p. 89
11. Ibid, p. 12
12. Ibid, p. 25
13. Pat [Timothy] O'Mara, *The Autobiography of a Liverpool Irish Slummy* (Bluecoat Press, Liverpool 1998) p. 57
14. Tom Paulin, quoted in 'Northern Protestants acting the part,' *Sunday Tribune* January 13 2002, p. 9
15. Joe Horgan, 'Oh to be in England now St. Patrick's here,' *Irish Post* March 10, 2003.
16. Paul Farrelly, quoted by Andrew Rawnsley on political profiles, www.guardian.co.uk.

17. Mick McCarthy, quoted in 'Irish ice makes Mick smile', by Jon Henderson, *The Observer*, September 9 2001, Sport section p. 6
18. *Evening Herald*, Friday May 24, 2002
19. Tom Humphries, 'One certainty-we're the poorer without Roy,' *The Irish Times*, May 27 2002 p. 10
20. Niall Quinn, *Niall Quinn: The Autobiography* (Headline, London 2002) p. 141
21. Jon Wiener, *Come Together-John Lennon in His Time* (Random House, New York 1984), p. 159
22. John Lennon and Yoko Ono, *Sunday Bloody Sunday*, from *Sometime in New York City* album, 1972.
23. Jon Wiener, op. cit., p. 208
24. Ellen Duncan, interview with author, July 20, 1999
25. Jon Wiener, op cit., p. 211
26. Deborah Frost, 'Once There Was a Way to Get Back Homeward...', *Record Magazine*, September 1984
27. Morrissey, in an interview with Brian Boyd, 'Paddy Englishman,' *The Irish Times* November 20, 1999
28. Richard Purden, 'Noel still gets a kick out of Celtic's wonderboys,' Irish Post, June 7, 2003 and Barry Egan, 'Mellowing Supernova', *The Irish Independent*, June 2, 2002.
29. Barry Egan, op. cit.
30. Olaf Tyaransen, Liam Gallagher interview, *Hot Press*, June 2002
31. All quotations from Elvis Costello in Neil McCormick, 'Elvis Unmasked' *Hot Press*, February 23, 1989
32. Phil Chevron, quoted in *If I Should Fall from the Grace of God, The Shane MacGowan Story* TG4 film broadcast March 2002.
33. Phil Chevron, quoted in 'Pogues Pogo On,' *Sunday Tribune*, May 19, 2002, p. 5
34. Shane MacGowan, quoted in *If I Should Fall from the Grace of God, The Shane MacGowan Story* TG4 film broadcast March 2002.
35. John Lydon Rotten, *No Blacks, No Irish, No Dogs* (Picador, New York, 1994), p. 9
36. Ibid, p. 27
37. Ibid, p. 28
38. Ibid, p. 20
39. Ibid, p. 99
40. Victoria Mary Clarke and Shane MacGowan, *A Drink With Shane MacGowan* (Sidgwick and Jackson, London 2001) and Johnny Rogan, 'Rebel yell,' *Irish Post* September 26, 1998
41. Johnny Rogan, op. cit.
42. John O'Neil, in sleeve notes from *The Best of: The Undertones* (1993). In fact the 1981 top 20 single *It's Gonna Happen* originally had lyrics about the Republican hunger strikes but the words were so 'shockingly cornball' said one band member that they were

rewritten with a less obviously political theme.

43. Malcolm Rogers, 'The accent on London Irish,' *Irish Post*, May 3, 2003, p. 18. See Paul Cunniffe, Excuse My Accent, 2003. See www.paulcunniffe.com

Chapter 2

1. Danny Morrison, 'Goon but not forgotten', *An Phoblacht/Republican News*, March 7, 2002
2. All quotes from Kevin Day, interview with author, March 16, 2002
3. Tony Geraghty, *The Irish War: The Military History of a Domestic Conflict* (HarperCollins, London 1998), p. xi
4. Ibid, p. 79
5. Ibid, p. 151
6. Martin McNamara, correspondence with author, March 13, 2003
7. Kevin Toolis, *Rebel Hearts-Journeys within the IRA's soul* (Picador, London 1995) p. 369
8. Ibid, p. 371
9. John Walsh, *The Falling Angels* (Flamingo, London 1999) p. 14
10. Pete McCarthy, *McCarthy's Bar* (Sceptre, London 2000) pp. 10-11
11. Ibid, p. 159
12. Pete McCarthy, interviewed on RTE 1 radio programme *Second Generation*, broadcast January 6, 2003
13. Conner, Rearden *Shake Hands With The Devil* (Literary Guild, New York, 1934) p. 29
14. Ibid, p. 36
15. Ibid, p. 241
16. David Lodge, *Ginger, You're Barmy* (Penguin 1987 edition, London: originally published in 1962) p. 31
17. Ibid, p. 203
18. Ibid, pp. 205 and 210
19. Robin Moore, *The Kaufman Snatch* (Manor, New York 1976) p. 9
20. Doris Lessing, *The Good Terrorist* (Jonathan Cape, London 1985), pp. 242, 304, 320 and 375
21. Morgan Llywelyn, *1916* (Tom Doherty Associates, New York 1998) p. 505
22. Jamie O'Neill, *At Swim, Two Boys* (Simon and Schuster, London 1997). The brothers' military careers are far from central to the main narrative to the plot, an excellent novel set in south Dublin during the prelude to the Easter Rising.
23. Ernie Nunan, 'The Kimmage Garrison, 1916' in *An t-Óglach*, Winter 1967
24. T. Ryle Dwyer, *Big Fellow, Long Fellow* (Gill and Macmillan, Dublin 1998) p. 75. For a more comprehensive account of the raid, see Piaras Béaslaí, *Michael Collins and the Making of a New Ireland* (Talbot, Dublin 1926) Vol I, p. 303.

25. Maud Gonne, MacBride's mother, was born near Aldershot in 1866 while her father was in the British Army. Gonne was brought up by a nurse in Ireland and then in Europe before moving back to Ireland aged 16 when her father was posted to Dublin. Mary MacSwiney, sister of famous Cork republican Terence MacSwiney, was born and educated in London. She trained as a teacher at Cambridge University. In 1914 MacSwiney was a founder member of Cumann na mBan and President of the Cork Branch for which she was interned after the 1916 Rising. She joined Sinn Féin in 1917 and in 1918 she was elected to the First Dáil for Cork. Appointed to the Cabinet of the Second Dáil in 1922 she was twice imprisoned during the Civil War, undergoing two hungerstrikes in prison in Kilmainham Gaol. After the Civil War MacSwiney remained active in Cumann na mBan and in republican politics. De Valera was born in New York to an Irish mother and Spanish father, though a 1921 memo from J. Edgar Hoover, special assistant to the US attorney general, bizarrely described him as a 'Portuguese Jew' in a report for the Justice Department's Bureau of Investigation. The background of other leading republicans is dealt with more fully later in the text.
26. Writing from Pearse, displayed at St Enda's School, Rathfarnham, Dublin. Display panel one.
27. Ruth Dudley Edwards, *Patrick Pearse, The Triumph of Failure* (Gollancz, London 1997) p. 175

Chapter 3

1. Joe Good, *Enchanted by Dreams* (Brandon, Dingle 1996) p. 24. Thomas M. Coffey, *Agony at Easter: The 1916 Rising* (London 1969) p. 4 recounts the same story but puts the number at 57 fares. Good himself was on the tram, and so I have used his recollection.
2. John T. O'Connor, 'Some Have Come From a Land Beyond The Sea,' *An t-Óglach*, Autumn 1966
3. Ibid, and Séamus Reader, 'Irishmen in Scotland,' *An t-Óglach,* Easter 1963
4. W.J. Brennan-Whitmore, *Dublin Burning* (Gill & Macmillan, Dublin 1996) pp. 36-38
5. John T. O'Connor, op. cit.
6. Kathleen Clarke, *Revolutionary Woman* (O'Brien, Dublin 1991) p. 67
7. Ibid, p. 95. There is some dispute over whether Clarke or Pearse was the first self-proclaimed president. Pearse read out the proclamation in the street, and history has often awarded him with the honour, but Clarke's case is at least as strong.
8. Desmond Ryan, *Michael Collins* (Anvil, Dublin 1932 [first published as The Invisible Army]), p. 11
9. Thomas Coffey, *Agony at Easter: The 1916 Rising*, p. 10 and Ruth

Dudley Edwards, *Patrick Pearse: The Triumph of Failure* (Gollancz, London 1977) p. 279
10. Margaret Skinnider, *Doing My Bit for Ireland* (Century, New York, 1917) pp. 3-9
11. Garrett Fitzgerald, interview with author, December 1, 2001
12. Desmond Fitzgerald, *Memoirs of Desmond Fitzgerald* (Routledge, London 1968) pp. 8-10 and Garrett Fitzgerald, *All in a Life* (Gill and Macmillan, Dublin 1991) p. 3
13. *Kerry's Fighting Story 1916-1921* (Kerryman Publications, Tralee 1966), p. 27
14. Desmond Fitzgerald, op. cit., p. 144
15. Joe Good, op. cit., p. 26
16. Ibid, p. 30
17. Ibid, p. 31
18. John T. O'Connor, op. cit.
19. Ibid, and Thomas Coffey, op. cit., pp. 64 and 101
20. Max Caulfield, *The Easter Rebellion* (Gill and Macmillan, Dublin 1963. 1995 edition), p. 98
21. Joe Good, op. cit., p. 32, and Sean Nunan, audio clip on http://www.bbc.co.uk/history/war/easterrising/radio/index_js.shtml.
22. Max Caulfield, op. cit., p. 131 and Peter de Rosa, *Rebels: The Irish Rising of 1916* (Poolbeg, Dublin 1990) p. 298
23. Joe Good, op. cit., p. 20. Collins had blatantly elbowed another runner, said Good. Collins ignored spectators' laughter and claimed victory.
24. F. X. Martin (ed) *The Irish Volunteers 1913-1915* (James Duffy, Dublin 1963) pp. 159 and 194
25. Joe Good, op. cit., p. 16. See also www.sivakalpa.org website for more information on Louis Noble.
26. Piaras Béaslaí, *Michael Collins and the Making of New Ireland* (Phoenix, Dublin 1926) p. 73. For Collins' life in London see also Tim Pat Coogan, *Michael Collins* (Hutchinson, London 1990) pp. 16-31.
27. Joe Good, op. cit., p. 35
28. Max Caulfield, op. cit, p. 168
29. W.J. Brennan-Whitmore, op. cit., p. 94
30. Elizabeth Coxhead, *Daughters of Erin* (Secker and Warburg, London 1965) p. 55
31. Max Caulfield, op. cit., p. 66
32. Margaret Skinnider, op. cit., p. 148
33. Ibid, p. 149
34. Ibid, p. 151
35. Max Caulfield, op. cit., p. 208, Peter de Rosa, op. cit., p.337 and Margaret Skinnider, op. cit., p. 148
36. Joe Good, op. cit., p. 45
37. Max Caulfield, op. cit., p. 260
38. Ibid, p. 232

39. Desmond Fitzgerald, op. cit., p. 144
40. Joe Good, op. cit., p. 57
41. C. Desmond Greaves, *The Life and Times of James Connolly* (Lawrence and Wishart, London 1961) pp. 20-24, and Emmett Larkin, *James Larkin: Irish Labour Leader 1876-1947* (Pluto, London 1989), p. 27
42 Joe Good, op. cit., p. 65
43. Max Caulfield, op. cit., p. 276
44 Joe Good, op. cit., p. 66
45. For accounts of the efforts to get the British-born to surrender, see Tim Pat Coogan, op. cit., p. 43, T. Ryle Dwyer, *Michael Collins: The Man Who Won The War* (Mercier, Dublin 1990), p. 26 and Joe Good, op. cit., pp. 66-68
46. Joe Good, op. cit., p. 70
47. C. Desmond Greaves, *Liam Mellows and the Irish Revolution* (Lawrence and Wishart, London 1971), p. 42
48. Margaret Skinnider, op. cit., p. 194
49. Desmond Fitzgerald, op. cit., p. 131, and Max Caulfield, op. cit., p. 99. On Hibernian Rifles, C. Desmond Greaves, *The Life and Times of James Connolly*, p. 410 says that 12 joined in on Easter Monday afternoon. Ruth Dudley Edwards, op. cit., p. 286 puts their eventual number at 30.
50. For a detailed exploration of de Valera's earliest years, see Tim Pat Coogan, *De Valera: Long Fellow, Long Shadow* (Hutchinson, London 1993) pp. 3-11
51. Ibid, p.78
52. C. Desmond Greaves, *The Life and Times of James Connolly*, pp. 20-24. Although the *County Press* and the *Isle of Wight News* both carried reports of the Sinn Féin Rising, both failed to make the local connection with the Rising's leader.
53. Piaras Béaslaí, op. cit., pp. 114-115
54. Joe Good, op. cit., p. 99 and *An t-Óglach*, St. Patrick's Day issue 1962, 'Attempts to Conscript Irish Prisoners,' by Ernest Nunan.

Chapter 4

1. See also www.sivakalpa.org website for more information on Louis Noble
2. John A. Pinkman, (ed. Francis Maguire), *In the Legion of the Vanguard* (Mercier, Cork, 1998) p. 25
3. Ibid, pp. 37-38
4. Ibid, p. 56
5. Peter Hart, 'Operations Abroad: The IRA in Britain, 1919-23,' *English Historical Review*, February 2000
6. Ibid
7. Ibid

8. Piaras Béaslaí, *Michael Collins and the Making of a New Ireland* (Talbot, Dublin 1926) Vol I, p. 303
9. Joe Good, *Enchanted by Dreams* (Brandon, Dingle 1996) p. 126
10. Ibid, pp. 130-134
11. Ibid, pp. 136-137
12. Ibid, p. 134
13. Ibid, pp. 173-175
14. Lord Longford, *Peace by Ordeal* (Cape, London 1935) p.102
15. Andrew Boyle, *The Riddle of Erskine Childers* (Hutchinson, London 1977) p. 245
16. Ibid, p. 250
17. Ibid, pp. 250 and 269
18. Ibid, pp. 277-280
19. Tim Pat Coogan, *Michael Collins* (Hutchinson, London 1990) p. 309

Chapter 5

1. Andrew Boyle, *The Riddle of Erskine Childers* (Hutchinson, London 1977) p. 304
2. Louis Noble transcribed interview on www.sivakalpa.org
3. John A. Pinkman (ed. Francis Maguire), *In the Legion of the Vanguard* (Mercier, Cork, 1998) p. 83
4. Ibid, p. 122
5. Ibid, p. 168
6. Among other possible assassins are Emmet Dalton (on Collins' side during the fight but who might have shot his commander through either incompetence, drunkenness or because he was a secret British agent), or IRA ambushers Robert Doherty, Mike Donoghue, Sean Galvin, Tom Hales, Jim Hurley, Pete Kearney (who told a priest before he died he thought he'd shot Collins), Tom Kelleher (blamed by Garda Sergeant John Hickey in his official enquiry of the death), Joe Murphy, Dan O'Connor, Denis 'Sonny' O'Neill (many researchers' favourite), Jimmy Ormond, and James Sheehan.
7. Meda Ryan, *The Day Michael Collins Was Shot* (Poolbeg, Dublin 1989) pp. 135-136
8. An anonymous note, apparently written by an eyewitness to Childers' execution, was made public in November 2002. See Michael Clifford, 'Eye-witness reveals details of Childers execution,' *Sunday Tribune* November 17 2002, p. 3.
9. John A. Pinkman, op. cit., pp. 193-194
10. Anthony J. Jordan, *Seán MacBride*, (Blackwater, Dublin 1993) p. 11
11. J. Bowyer Bell, *The Secret Army: The IRA 1916-1979* (Poobeg, Dublin 1990 edition), p. 130
12. Anthony J. Jordan, op. cit., p. 67
13. *The Times*, February 24, 1939
14. *The Times*, April 4, 1939

15. *The Times*, February 24, 1939
16. *The Times*, February 24, 1939
17. C. Desmond Greaves, 'Reminiscences of the Connolly Association' (Emerald Jubilee Pamphlet, 1978)
18. Richard Doherty, *Irish Volunteers in the Second World War* (Four Courts Press, Dublin 2002) p. 92
19. Ibid, p. 141
20. Mahr's Irland-Redaktion Blueprint, printed as Appendix 1 in David O'Donoghue, *Hitler's Irish Voices* (Beyond the Pale, Belfast 1998) p. 185
21. Ibid
22. David O'Donoghue, op. cit., p. xviii
23. Ibid, p. 54

Chapter 6

1. Seán MacStiofáin, interview with author, July 4, 2000
2. Seán MacStiofáin, interview with author, May 29, 2000
3. Seán MacStiofáin, interview with author, July 4, 2000
4. Seán MacStiofáin, interview with author, May 29, 2000 and Seán MacStiofáin, *Revolutionary in Ireland* (Gordon Cremonesi, Edinburgh 1975), p. 21
5. Seán MacStiofáin, op. cit., pp. 20-22
6. Ibid, pp. 27-28 and Seán MacStiofáin, interview with author, May 29, 2000
7. Seán MacStiofáin, interview with author, May 29, 2000
8. Seán MacStiofáin, op. cit., p. 40 and Seán MacStiofáin, interview with author, July 4, 2000
9. Seán MacStiofáin, in inteview with RTÉ television some time in early 1980s. Interview was broadcast soon after MacStiofáin death in May 2001.
10. Seán MacStiofáin, op. cit., p. 47
11. Ibid, p. 12
12. Seán MacStiofáin, interviews with author, May 29, 2000 and July 4, 2000
13. *Felsted News*, May 2001.
14. Seán MacStiofáin, op. cit., p. 2
15. Ibid, p. 13
16. Seán MacStiofáin, interview with author, July 4, 2000
17. Ibid
18. Ibid
19. Ibid
20. Seán MacStiofáin, op. cit., p. 86.
21. All quotations from Seán Ó Ceallacháin, interview with author, July 22, 2002

22. Justin O'Brien, *The Arms Trial* (Gill and Macmillan, Dublin 2000) p. 19
23. Seán MacStiofáin, quoted in Justin O'Brien, op. cit., p. 21
24. Cathal Goulding, quoted in Patrick Bishop and Eamonn Mallie, *The Provisional IRA* (Heinemann, London 1987) p. 86
25. Richard Deutsch and Vivien Magowan, *Northern Ireland: A Chronology of Events 1968-1973* (Belfast: Blackstaff, 1973) Vol.1, p. 17
26. Quoted BBC TV 'Timewatch' documentary, *The Sparks That Lit The Bonfire*, 1993
27. Ibid
28. Martin Meehan, interview with author, May 27, 1996
29. Tomas MacGiolla, quoted in Bishop and Mallie, op. cit., p. 94 and Tomas Mac Giolla, interview with author, July 31, 1996
30. Ruari Ó Bradaigh, quoted in Bishop and Mallie, op. cit., p. 136

Chapter 7

1. Seán MacStiofáin, quoted in Rosita Sweetman, *On Our Knees* (Pan, London 1972) p. 160
2. Richard Rose, *Governing Without Consensus*, p. 109 and see Patrick Bishop and Eamonn Mallie, *The Provisional IRA*, pp. 128-132, and J. Bowyer Bell, The Troubles, pp. 157-161
3. All other quotations from Seán MacStiofáin in this chapter, interview with author, July 4, 2000
4. Peter Taylor, *Brits: The War Against the IRA* (Bloomsbury, London 2001) p. 84 and Seán MacStiofáin, interview with author, July 4, 2000
5. Seán MacStiofáin, interview with author, July 4, 2000, and Seán MacStiofáin, quoted in Peter Taylor, *Behind the Mask: The IRA and Sinn Fein* (TV Books, New York 1997), p. 169
6. Frank Steele, quoted in Peter Taylor, op. cit., p. 169
7. See Joe Cahill, *A Life in the IRA* (O'Brien, Dublin 2002) p. 259
8. *Irish Post*, Saturday December 2, 1972, p. 1
9. Pat Doherty, interview with author, December 19, 2002
10. Ibid
11. As quoted in Patrick Magee, *Gangsters or Guerrillas: Representations of Irish Republicans in 'Troubles Fiction'* (Beyond the Pale, Belfast 2001) p. 103
12. *Sunday Times*, May 5 1985 'Provos' ex-chief was a police informer', p. 1
13. Staff reporter, *Irish News*, 'Republicans united in grief', May 22, 2001
14. David McKittrick, *The Independent*, May 18, 2001
15. Ibid
16. Martin Cowley, 'London-born IRA chief Sean MacStiofáin dies,' Reuters newswire May 18, 2001

17. 'Provisional IRA leader, dies at 73,' Associated Press (appeared in *Washington Post* May 20, 2001)
18. John Manley, 'IRA man was not informer,' *Irish News* May 21, 2001
19. Bloody Sunday transcript, May 21, 2001
20. Kevin Myers, 'An Irishman's Diary,' *The Irish Times* May 22, 2001
21. Ibid
22. All quotations from 'Onlooker', *Derry Journal*, July 3. 2001
23. Manus Canning, letter in *Derry Journal*, August 2001
24. Ibid

Chapter 8

1. *Irish Post*, Saturday November 30, 1974 p.1
2. *The Times*, Friday November 22, 1974 p.1
3. Gary Kent, 'Kevin Barry Curran: a rebel with a cause,' *Irish Post*, April 26, 2003 p. 6
4. C. Desmond Greaves, 'Reminiscences of the Connolly Association' (Emerald Jubilee Pamphlet, 1978)
5. All quotations from Clare Short, interview on *Second Generation*, RTE 1 radio programme, broadcast January 13, 2003
6. Blake Morrison, interviewed on *Second Generation*, RTE 1 radio programme, broadcast February 10, 2003
7. All quotations from Mark Wogan, interview on *Second Generation*, RTE 1 radio programme, broadcast January 20, 2003
8. Paddy Hillyard, *Suspect Community: People's Experience of the Prevention of Terrorism Acts in Britain* (Pluto, London 1993) p. 259
9. All quotations from Margaret Brady, interview with author, September 30, 2002
10. All quotations from Vince Maguire, interview with author, January 2, 2003
11. Pat Maguire, interview with author, January 2, 2003
12. John Maguire, interview with author, March 24, 2003
13. Anne Maguire, *Miscarriage of Justice: An Irish Family's Story of Wrongful Conviction as IRA Terrorists* (Roberts Rinehart, Colorado 1994) p. 14
14. Robert Kee, *Trial and Error* (Hamish Hamilton, London 1986) pp. 96-97.
15. John Maguire, interview with author, March 24, 2003
16. Pat Maguire, interview with author, January 2, 2002
17. Anne Maguire, op. cit., p. 19
18. Vince Maguire, interview with author, January 2, 2003
19. Pat Maguire, interview with author, January 2, 2003 and John Maguire, interview with author, March 24, 2003
20. Vince Maguire, interview with author, January 2, 2003
21. Ibid
22. John Maguire, interview with author, March 24, 2003

23. Ibid
24. *The Times*, Friday March 5, 1974 p. 1
25. Ibid, p. 2.
26. John Maguire, interview with author, March 24, 2003

Chapter 9

1. All quotations from Pat Maguire, interview with author, January 2, 2003
2. All quotations from Vince Maguire, interview with author, January 2, 2003. Paul Norney was sentenced to life in prison when he was 17.
3. All quotations from John Maguire, interview with author, March 24, 2003
4. Vince and Pat Maguire, interviews with author, January 2, 2003
5. Anne Maguire, *Miscarriage of Justice: An Irish Family's Story of Wrongful Conviction as IRA Terrorists* (Roberts Rinehart, Colorado 1994) p. 33
6. Ibid, p. 44
7. Ibid, p. 11
8. All quotations from Jim Doherty, correspondence with author, April 23, 2003. *Sean South from Garryowen* in fact commemorates an IRA raid in 1957, in which South died. Although well after 1916, it is still essentially an historical ballad from an era before the modern Troubles.
9. Conor Foley, quoted as case 371/M 85 in Paddy Hillyard, *Suspect Community: People's Experience of the Prevention of Terrorism Acts in Britain* (Pluto, London 1993) p. 156
10. All quotations from Conor Foley, correspondence with author, November 8, 2002
11. *South London Press*, 15 November, 1985
12. Paddy Hillyard, correspondence with author, August 19, 2002 and Paddy Hillyard, op. cit., p. 1. See also Gearoid O'Meachair 'A Diplomatic Blind Eye, A Catalogue of Neglect,' London, February 1996, quoted in Tim Pat Coogan, *Wherever Green is Worn* (Hutchinson, London 2000) p.149
13. *The Times* Wednesday December 7, 1988

Chapter 10

1. Simon O'Hagan, 'I can understand why a young Muslim man would do what Omar is meant to have done,' *Independent on Sunday*, May 4, 2003, p.21. In fact, Omar Khan Sharif was accompanied by another British Muslim suicide bomber, Asif Mohammed Hanif.
2. All quotations from Reg Tester, submission to Bloody Sunday (Saville) Inquiry. Part of statement read at Inquiry on April 5, 2000

3. Grant McKee and Ros Franey, *Time Bomb: Irish Bombers, English Justice and the Guildford Four* (Bloomsbury, London 1988) p. 191
4. Matt Seaton, 'Red Army Faction', *The Independent on Sunday,* January 25, 1995.
5. Seán MacStiofáin, interview with author, July 4, 2000
6. All quotations from Michael Gallagher, interview with author, August 18, 2002
7. John Steele, '20 Years for "Sleeper" who helped in attack on Heathrow,' *Daily Telegraph*, February 28, 1998
8. All quotations from Paddy Kelly, interview with author, November 13, 2002
9. Sean O'Mahony, *Frongoch: University of Revolution* (FDR Teoranta, Dublin 1987), p. 47
10. Shane O'Neill, quoted in BBC TV Spotlight programme *Death of an IRA Quartermaster*, shown March 2000
11. David Millward, Toby Harnden and John Steele, 'IRA suspect killed in raid went to school in London' *Daily Telegraph* September 25, 1997
12, Ibid, and Paddy Kelly, interview with author, November 13, 2002
13. Toby Harnden, 'Irish roots drew him to rebel cause,' *Daily Telegraph*, September 25, 1996 and *An Phoblacht/Republican News*, October 2, 1996
14. Jimmy Murphy, interview with author, July 3, 2003
15. Diarmuid O'Neill, quoted in BBC TV 'Spotlight' programme *Death of an IRA Quartermaster*, shown March 2000
16. Police recording from BBC TV 'Spotlight' programme *Death of an IRA Quartermaster*, shown March 2000
17. 'Kilo', quoted in ibid
18. Brian McHugh, quoted in ibid
19. Shane O'Neill, quoted in ibid
20. Michael Hornsell, 'IRA man may have been unarmed,' *The Times*, September 25, 1996
21. Karmele Erono, quoted in BBC TV 'Spotlight' programme, op. cit.
22. Oliver Donohue, quoted in ibid
23. Grant McKee and Ros Franey, op. cit., p. 229
24. Ibid, p. 17
25. Irish Republican Socialist Movement website, 'Dying Irish Republican Honored' October 16, 1996
26. Grant McKee and Ros Franey, op. cit., p. 199
27. Ibid, p. 327
28. *The Times*, February 11, 1977 p. 4
29. Gerry Adams, quoted in Ed Moloney, *A Secret History of the IRA* (Allen Lane, London 2002) p. 480

Chapter 11

1. All quotations from Pat Doherty, interview with author, December 19, 2002
2. See Ed Moloney, *A Secret History of the IRA* (Allen Lane, London 2002) pp. 397-398, 479
3. Correspondence with Kieran Clifford, July 3, 2003
4. All quotations from Theresa Moriarty, interview with author, August 27, 2002

Chapter 12

1. Edward Casey (ed. by Joanna Burke), *The Misfit Soldier* (Cork University Press, Cork 1999), p. 4
2. Ibid, pp. 27-28
3. Ibid, p. 60
4. Jimmy Johnson, 'Their Country's Reward,' unpublished manuscript, quoted in John Lindsay, *Brits Speak Out* (Guildhall, Derry 1998) p. 68
5. Nicky Curtis, *Faith and Duty: The True Story of a Soldier's War in Northern Ireland* (André Deutsch, London 1998) p. 19
6. Ibid, p. 23
7. Ibid, pp. 46-47
8. Ibid, p. 170
9. John Parker, *Death of a Hero: Captain Robert Nairac, GC and the undercover war in Northern Ireland* (Metro, London 1999) p. 1
10. Ibid, p. 168
11. Ibid, p. 223
12. Ibid, p. 166 and Toby Harnden, *Bandit Country: The IRA and South Armagh* (Hodder and Stoughton, London 1999) p. 296
13. Nicky Curtis, op. cit., p. 296
14. Bert Henshaw, quoted in John Lindsay, op. cit., p. 13
15. Ibid, p. 14
16. 'James', quoted in John Lindsay, op. cit., pp. 89-90
17. Bernard O'Mahoney, *Soldier of the Queen* (Brandon, Dingle 2000), p. 27
18. Ibid, p. 41
19. Ibid, p. 28
20. Captain Dale Clarke RA, Directorate of Corporate Communications (Army), correspondence with author, July 8, 2002
21. Bernard O'Mahoney, op. cit., p. 124
22. Ibid, p. 131
23. Ibid, p. 132
24. Ibid, p. 235
25. Ibid, p. 247

26. Gerry Conlon, quoted in Grant McKee and Ros Franey, *Time Bomb: Irish Bombers, English Justice and the Guildford Four* (Bloomsbury, London 1988) p.110 and Paul Hill, *Stolen Years* (Doubleday, London 1990) p. 125
27. Gerry Conlon, *Proved Innocent* (Hamish Hamilton, London 1990) p.79
28. Interview with Patrick Kelly, November 13, 2002
29. Martin Dillon, *Stone Cold: The True Story of Michael Stone and the Milltown Massacre* (Hutchinson, London 1992) p. 11. In 1995 loyalist sympathiser Jason Campbell knifed and killed 16 year-old Celtic supporter Mark Scott in Glasgow. Campbell was a native of Glasgow, his father and uncle were past members of the UVF, and the attack was widely regarded as sectarian. Although the killing was apparently not part of a loyalist campaign, Campbell asked to be transferred to the Maze Prison to join the UVF prisoners there. The British government originally agreed to the request, and then changed its mind in the face of forceful criticism.
30. Ibid, p. 21
31. Eamon Collins, *Killing Rage* (Granta, London 1997) p. 88
32. Ibid, p. 357
33. Tony Blair, quoted in Paddy Logue (ed.) *Being Irish* (Oak Tree Press, Dublin 2000) p.12
34. Tony Blair's speech to the Royal Ulster Agricultural Show, May 16, 1997

Chapter 13

1. O'Donovan Rossa, *Irish Rebels in English Prisons* (Brandon, Dingle 1991) p. 163 and 177
2. Brian O'Higgins 'From a Land Beyond the Wave', in *Easter 1916: The Story of the Rising* (Talbot, Dublin 1966) p. 57
3. Maurice Good, in Joe Good, *Enchanted by Dreams* (Brandon, Dingle 1996) p. 188
4. Anthony Jordan, *Seán MacBride* (Blackwater, Dublin 1993) p. 84
5. Seán MacBride, introduction to Bobby Sands, *One Day in My Life* (Pluto, London 1982) p. 18
6. Kathleen Clarke, *Revolutionary Woman* (O'Brien, Dublin 1991) pp. 69-70
7. Ibid, p. 144
8. *Washington Post*, September 8, 1981 p. A-16
9. Garret Fitzgerald, 'What happened to Good Friday?' *London Review of Books*, September 2, 1999
10. Garret Fitzgerald, quoted on BBC History website http://www.bbc.co.uk/history/war/easterrising/personal/index.shtml
11. Bill Flynn, quoted in Conor O'Clery, *Daring Diplomacy* (Roberts Rinehart, Colorado) p. 53
12. Bill Flynn, quoted in Eamonn Mallie and David McKittrick, *The Fight for Peace* (Heinemann, London 1996) p. 281

13. Bill Flynn, quoted in Conor O'Clery, op. cit., p. 154
14. For the summary of the legalities of citizenship, and the Supreme Court rulings, I draw heavily on Ursula Fraser's unpublished paper 'Two–Tier Citizenship–the Lobe and Osayande Case' presented at Women's Movement: Migrant Women Transforming Ireland conference, Trinity College, Dublin March 20-21, 2003
15. Frank McCourt, *'Tis*, (Scribner, New York 1999) p. 212

Bibliography

Newspapers/Journals

An t-Óglach
An Phoblacht/Republican News
British Medical Journal
Daily Telegraph
Derry Journal
English Historical Review
Evening Herald
Felsted News
Hot Press
The Independent
The Independent on Sunday
The Irish Independent
Irish Journal of Sociology
Irish News
Irish Post
The Irish Times
Isle of Wight County Press
Isle of Wight News
London Review of Books
New York Times
The Observer
Sunday Times
Sunday Tribune
The Times
Washington Post

Books

Anderson, Brendan *Joe Cahill: A Life in the IRA* (O'Brien, Dublin 2002)
Béaslaí, Piaras *Michael Collins and the Making of a New Ireland* (Talbot, Dublin 1926)
Bell, J. Bowyer *The Secret Army: The IRA 1916-1979* (Poolbeg, Dublin 1990 edition)
Bishop, Patrick and Eamonn Mallie *The Provisional IRA* (Heinemann, London 1987)
Boyle, Andrew *The Riddle of Erskine Childers* (Hutchinson, London 1977)
Brennan-Whitmore, W.J. *Dublin Burning* (Gill and Macmillan, Dublin 1996)
Casey, Edward (ed. by Joanna Burke), *The Misfit Soldier* (Cork University Press, Cork 1999)
Caulfield, Max *The Easter Rebellion* (Gill and Macmillan, Dublin 1963. 1995 edition)
Clarke, Kathleen *Revolutionary Woman* (O'Brien, Dublin 1991)
Clarke, Victoria Mary and Shane MacGowan *A Drink With Shane MacGowan* (Sidgwick and Jackson, London 2001)
Coffey, Thomas M. *Agony at Easter: The 1916 Rising* (Pelican, Harmondsworth 1971)
Collins, Eamon *Killing Rage* (Granta, London 1997)
Conlon, Gerry *Proved Innocent* (Hamish Hamilton, London 1990)
Conner, Rearden *Shake Hands With The Devil* (Literary Guild, New York, 1934)
Coogan, Tim Pat *Michael Collins* (Hutchinson, London 1990)
Coogan, Tim Pat *De Valera: Long Fellow, Long Shadow* (Hutchinson, London 1993)
Coogan, Tim Pat *Wherever Green is Worn* (Hutchinson, London 2000)
Coxhead, Elizabeth *Daughters of Erin* (Secker and Warburg, London 1965)
Curtis, Nicky *Faith and Duty: The True Story of a Soldier's War in Northern Ireland* (André Deutsch, London 1998)
de Rosa, Peter *Rebels: The Irish Rising of 1916* (Poolbeg, Dublin 1990)
Dillon, Martin *Stone Cold: The True Story of Michael Stone and the Milltown Massacre* (Hutchinson, London 1992)
Deutsch, Richard and Vivien Magowan, *Northern Ireland: A Chronology of Events 1968-1973* (Belfast, Blackstaff, 1973)
Doherty, Richard *Irish Volunteers in the Second World War* (Four Courts Press, Dublin 2002)
Dwyer, T. Ryle *Michael Collins: The Man Who Won The War* (Mercier, Dublin 1990)
Dwyer, T. Ryle *Big Fellow, Long Fellow* (Gill and Macmillan, Dublin 1998)
Dudley Edwards, Ruth *Patrick Pearse, The Triumph of Failure* (Gollancz, London 1977)

Fitzgerald, Desmond *Memoirs of Desmond Fitzgerald* (Routledge, London 1968)

Fitzgerald, Garrett *All in a Life* (Gill and Macmillan, Dublin 1991)

Geraghty, Tony *The Irish War: The Military History of a Domestic Conflict* (HarperCollis, London 1998)

Good, Joe *Enchanted by Dreams* (Brandon, Dingle 1996)

Greaves, C. Desmond *The Life and Times of James Connolly* (Lawrence and Wishart, London 1961)

Greaves, C. Desmond *Liam Mellows and the Irish Revolution* (Lawrence and Wishart, London 1971)

Hillyard, Paddy *Suspect Community: People's Experience of the Prevention of Terrorism Acts in Britain* (Pluto, London 1993)

Jordan, Anthony J.*Seán MacBride* (Blackwater, Dublin 1993)

Kee, Robert *Trial and Error* (Hamish Hamilton, London 1986)

Kerry's Fighting Story 1916-1921 (Kerryman Publications, Tralee 1966)

Larkin, Emmett *James Larkin: Irish Labour Leader 1876-1947* (Pluto, London 1989)

Lessing, Doris *The Good Terrorist* (Jonathan Cape, London 1985)

Lindsay, John *Brits Speak Out* (Guildhall, Derry 1998)

Llywelyn, Morgan *1916* (Tom Doherty Associates, New York 1998)

Lodge, David *Ginger, You're Barmy* (Penguin 1987 edition, London: originally published in 1962)

Logue, Paddy (ed.) *Being Irish* (Oak Tree Press, Dublin 2000)

Lord Longford, *Peace by Ordeal* (Cape, London 1935)

MacStiofáin, Seán *Revolutionary in Ireland* (Gordon Cremonesi, Edinburgh 1975)

Magee, Patrick *Gangsters or Guerrillas: Representations of Irish Republicans in 'Troubles Fiction'* (Beyond the Pale, Belfast 2001)

Maguire, Anne *Miscarriage of Justice: An Irish Family's Story of Wrongful Conviction as IRA Terrorists* (Roberts Rinehart, Colorado 1994)

Mallie, Eamonn and David McKittrick *The Fight for Peace* (Heinemann, London 1996)

Martin, F. X. (ed) *The Irish Volunteers 1913-1915* (James Duffy, Dublin 1963)

McCarthy, Pete *McCarthy's Bar* (Sceptre, London 2000)

McCourt, Frank *Tis* (Scribner, New York 1999)

McKee, Grant and Ros Franey *Time Bomb: Irish Bombers, English Justice and the Guildford Four* (Bloomsbury, London 1988)

Moloney, Ed *A Secret History of the IRA* (Allen Lane, London 2002)

Moore, Robin *The Kaufman Snatch* (Manor, New York 1976)

O'Brien, Justin *The Arms Trial* (Gill and Macmillan, Dublin 2000)

O'Clery, Conor *Daring Diplomacy* (Roberts Rinehart, Colorado)

O'Donoghue, David *Hitler's Irish Voices. The Story of German Radio's Wartime Irish Service* (Beyond the Pale, Belfast 1998)

O'Mahoney, Bernard *Soldier of the Queen* (Brandon, Dingle 2000)
O'Mahony, Sean *Frongoch: University of Revolution* (FDR Teoranta, Dublin 1987)
O'Mara, Pat [Timothy] *The Autobiography of a Liverpool Irish Slummy* (Bluecoat Press, Liverpool 1998)
O'Neill, Jamie *At Swim, Two Boys* (Simon and Schuster, London 1997)
Parker, John *Death of a Hero: Captain Robert Nairac, GC and the Undercover War in Northern Ireland* (Metro, London 1999)
Pinkman, John A. (ed. Francis Maguire) *In the Legion of the Vanguard* (Mercier, Cork 1998)
Quinn, Niall *Niall Quinn: The Autobiography* (Headline, London 2002)
O'Donovan Rossa, Jeremiah *Irish Rebels in English Prisons* (Brandon, Dingle 1991)
Rotten, John Lydon *No Blacks, No Irish, No Dogs* (Picador, New York 1994)
Ryan, Desmond *Michael Collins* (Anvil, Dublin 1932 [first published as The Invisible Army])
Ryan, Meda *The Day Michael Collins Was Shot* (Poolbeg, Dublin 1989)
Sands, Bobby *One Day in My Life* (Pluto, London 1982)
Skinnider, Margaret *Doing My Bit for Ireland* (Century, New York, 1917)
Sweetman, Rosita *On Our Knees* (Pan, London 1972)
Taylor, Peter *Behind the Mask: The IRA and Sinn Fein* (TV Books, New York 1997)
Taylor, Peter *Brits: The War Against the IRA* (Bloomsbury, London 2001)
Toolis, Kevin *Rebel Hearts-Journeys within the IRA's Soul* (Picador, London 1995)
Walsh, John *The Falling Angels* (Flamingo, London 1999)
Wiener, Jon *Come Together-John Lennon in His Time* (Random House, New York 1984)